From

The Women's Press Ltd
124 Shoreditch High Street, London E1

The London Rape Crisis Centre runs a 24-hour counselling line, offering legal and medical information and emotional support to women and girls who have been raped or sexually assaulted. The centre opened in 1976 and is run by and for women.

London RCC
PO Box 69
London WC1X 9NJ

Telephone: 01 837 1600 (24 hours)
     01 278 3956 (office)

LONDON RAPE CRISIS CENTRE

[Sexual Violence]
The Reality for Women

The Women's Press Handbook Series

First published by The Women's Press Limited 1984
A member of the Namara Group
124 Shoreditch High Street, London E1 6JE

British Library Cataloguing in Publication Data

The London Rape Crisis Centre
    Sexual violence.–(The Women's Press handbook series)
    1. Rape
    I. Title
    364.1′532   HV6558

    ISBN 0-7043-3910-2

Typeset by MC Typeset, Chatham, Kent
Printed in Great Britain by Nene Litho
and bound by Woolnough Bookbinding
both of Wellingborough, Northants

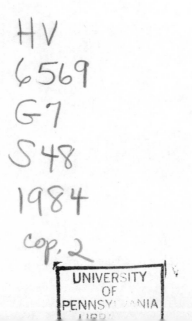

Contents

Acknowledgements

We would like to acknowledge Carol Ann Hooper, Bernardette Manning and Jennifer Peck who wrote the book; Hannah Kanter who edited it; and Ann Jessup, Barrister, Fay Hutchinson, Medical Director of the Brook Advisory Centre, Oonagh Watters, Medical Doctor at the Westminster Venereal Diseases Clinic, and Claudia Granger-Taylor, Medical Doctor, for their careful advice.

We also acknowledge all the women who have ever been involved with or contacted the London Rape Crisis Centre, because it is from their experiences, energy and ideas that this book has come.

The London Rape Crisis Centre Collective

Preface

It is difficult for women to speak about experiences of sexual violence. Society perpetuates a hostile silence which denies reality for women who have been raped. In the Women's Liberation Movement we have learnt that talking and working together to break this silence can be enormously strengthening. The London Rape Crisis Centre was opened in 1976 by a group of women who had been talking in this way about rape. It is run by and for women. (There are now many other rape crisis centres in the UK. Each group was set up separately and each remains autonomous.) Our primary aim is to provide a place where women and girls who have been raped or sexually assaulted can talk with other women, at any time of the day or night.

Unlike most agencies that women came into contact with, we always believe any woman who calls us. We also offer emotional support and/or legal and medical information according to what each woman wishes. We are also committed to educating and informing the public about the reality of rape, to refute the many myths and misconceptions which distort and deny women's experiences.

This book is an attempt to inform women about rape and sexual assault. It is intended to share with women the knowledge and experience we have gained over the years about rape, why it exists, and what effect it has on us. We describe the legal and medical processes in which women become involved after being raped, since it is important to be able to make informed decisions about how to act.

Rape is not confined to forcible penetration of a woman's vagina by a man's penis. It is all the sexual assaults, verbal and physical, that we all suffer in our daily contact with men. These range from being 'touched up' or 'chatted up' to being brutally sexually assaulted with objects. Throughout this book we use the word 'rape' to describe any kind of sexual assault.

We have referred to the assailant throughout as 'the man'. We know of course that very often there is more than one man involved in an attack, and that men or boys of any age are capable of, and do, rape women of any age.

The word 'victim' does not appear in this book. It does not adequately describe women who are part of and who have contacted the London Rape Crisis Centre. Rape does affect women for some time after it happens, but it often unleashes anger that has never been able to find its target before, which is strengthening. There is not a separate category of women who are 'victims' just as there is no category of men who are 'rapists'. Using the word 'victim' to describe women takes away our power and contributes to the idea that it is right and natural for men to 'prey' on us.

Sexual Violence

1
Myths and Realities

Rape is a subject which people find uncomfortable. For women it conjures up all kinds of images. Some of us will think of dirty old men in plastic coats, or monsters too grotesque to think about. Others will have more specific ideas about rape; perhaps thinking about a certain group of men such as 'lunatics' in dark alleys.

Every woman in our society feels the fear of rape – no woman is allowed to ignore it. We are taught as little girls to be afraid of 'strange men' who offer us sweets, lifts, anything. We are taught as adults to keep our doors locked, not to be alone, not to look or act in any way that might 'bring rape upon ourselves'. Perhaps the most obvious situation in which we are taught to be afraid is when we walk alone at night. We must always be careful, always be aware that rape is a possibility. This fear is reinforced in every part of our lives because we are constantly threatened and intimidated by men. Think of being in any crowded place – on public transport or in a crowded hall. Most women will have experienced men pushing up against us in an uncomfortable manner and will have been unable to do anything about it other than get away as soon as possible. All the harassment we endure, from men whistling at us as we pass building sites to a boss at work who will not take his eyes or hands off our bodies, is part of the process of intimidation which ends with rape. With every comment on our bodies, every leer, men are letting us know, quite clearly, that they have access to our bodies and that we have no control over that access. They are saying, in effect, 'if I choose, I can rape you – so make sure you don't antagonise me'.

We are taught to avoid rape. Everyone has a prescription for this. They range from being a karate expert to dressing 'sensibly'. *None* of them work completely. Doing a self-defence course may make you feel more confident about your ability to defend yourself physically – it may not help if the man has a weapon, and will not if you are in an enclosed space, or if you go into shock and 'freeze'. As for clothes – if a man decides to rape you, what you are wearing will make no difference.

We are told that if we behave in certain ways we will avoid being raped. We must not threaten men by being too assertive – if we do they will want to take us down a peg or two. On the other hand, we must not act as though we cannot take care of ourselves – this will encourage men to take advantage of our helplessness. We must not live alone or with other women – that encourages men to rape us because we are obviously not protected by a man. On the other hand, husbands have every right to rape their wives. Rape in marriage is not a crime and it is virtually impossible to bring a charge of rape against any man you live with. Avoiding walking alone at night – especially in badly-lit areas – is another favourite prescription for avoiding rape. However, being indoors at night (or during the day) can be equally dangerous – about 50 percent[1] of rapes are carried out either in the man's home or in the woman's. The list of rules is endless. If you are raped you can be sure that you (and everyone you tell) will be able to find numerous rules that you have broken, or numerous things that you might have done to avoid it or stop it happening. Many women never realise that rape does not 'happen', it is caused – by men. Men commit a particular crime against women and the only person who is responsible for that crime is the man who commits it. The rules we are given to avoid rape serve only to shift the responsibility from *men* on to us; to make us feel guilty for men's crime against us. They are also there to control our movements; restrict our freedom. We live in this society as though we were in a state of siege and what's more, we are made to feel as though we were responsible for that state of affairs.

How to avoid rape[2]

Don't go out without clothes – that encourages some men
Don't go out with clothes – any clothes encourage some men
Don't go out alone at night – that encourages men

Don't go out alone at any time – any situation encourages some men

Don't go out with a female friend – some men are encouraged by numbers

Don't go out with a male friend – some male friends are capable of rape

Don't stay at home – intruders and relatives can both rape

Avoid childhood – some rapists are 'turned on' by little girls

Avoid old age – some rapists 'prefer' aged women

Don't have a father, grandfather, uncle or brother – these are the relatives who most often rape young women

Don't have neighbours – these often rape women

Don't marry – rape is legal within marriage

To be quite sure – don't exist

As well as being given very strict rules and codes of behaviour in order to avoid rape, women are exposed to jokes, fictional stories and media reports of rape which all describe the crime in a way that is different from reality; they incorporate many myths which are designed to take away responsibility from men and to obscure the reality of the experience of being raped.

For example, there is a widely held belief that women enjoy rape. It is, after all, 'just sex when we don't want it'. Rape is a crime of sexual violence and humiliation which can involve beating, physical restraint, the use of knives and sticks, urinating and defecating. Studies have consistently shown that most rapes involve physical force to some degree. Often when a woman is raped she is afraid that she will be killed – men often use the threat of killing a woman or her children to ensure her 'submission' and her silence after the event. Women *do not* enjoy this.

Another myth that many people believe to be true is that 'rape is an act committed by a maniac'. The fact is that very few convicted rapists are referred for psychiatric treatment, because attempts to find something to treat have been singularly unsuccessful. Many rapists have normal scores on tests for aggression and attitudes towards women. In 1980 in England and Wales only 2 percent of men

Maniac myth (handwritten)

convicted of rape were referred for psychiatric treatment.[3] This myth is a particularly comfortable one for women to believe. If a rapist is a lunatic, then he will be recognisable and therefore avoidable. It also immunises all the 'normal' men a woman might know and trust from the possibility of being rapists. It gives us the illusion that we are safe and stops us being completely paralysed with fear – or stops our anger at what men do to us from becoming too powerful. In this way men get access to women and rape women with impunity because we are not 'cautious' enough about them. We trust them with our daughters – and they frequently abuse that trust too. Seventy-five percent of men who sexually assault girls are known to and trusted by both the girl and her family.[4]

certain women only myth (handwritten)

The illusion that we are safe is also contained in the myth that 'only certain types of women get raped'. This is not true. Over the past five years the London RCC has been contacted by or on behalf of women and girls of all ages (from 3 years old to 90 years old); all classes; all races. Many women believe that if they are not part of a certain category of women they are safe from being raped. As with the 'maniac' myth, this one enables us to feel immune (to a large extent – unless we break one of the rules) from rape.

Rapists are not, as is also commonly believed, in the grip of an 'uncontrollable sexual urge'. From various studies we know that over 80 percent of rapes are wholly or partially planned in advance.[5] All rapes committed by more than one assailant are always planned. Men can quite easily control their urges to have sex – they do not need to rape a woman to satisfy them. This idea that men are so weak-willed as to have to rape every time they get a sexual urge is designed to do two things. Firstly it is designed to make women (who supposedly cause this sexual urge) responsible for rapes committed against us and secondly to make sure that women do not deny men access to our bodies when they are sexually aroused because if we do, then they will be forced to 'go out and rape a woman' – or even a child.

Our supposed responsibility in this crime is illustrated again in the idea that women 'ask for' or 'deserve' rape. The idea is that any woman who breaks established rules of conduct – by hitchhiking, walking alone, inviting men into her house, being more articulate than her boyfriend, being more competent than a male colleague at

*+ those opinions are a
bit extreme on fem. side*

her work – the list is endless – ought to be punished by whatever man she has trusted or offended. This punishment is rape. *x*

Reporting to the police will bring you face to face with another myth – that women make false and malicious allegations of rape against innocent men. This is untrue. There was an experiment carried out in the New York Police Force in the early 1970s. A rape squad was set up comprising women officers only. All allegations of rape went to this squad and they would begin (as they would with any other crime) by believing the woman reporting. It was found that the percentage of allegations of rape that were false was exactly the same as that for other crimes – 2 percent.[6] (Previous to this the 'false allegation' rate was said to be 15 percent.) In this country the police *ENGLAND. not U.S.* start with the assumption that women who report being raped are lying. Many women do not get past the desk – even though what they are reporting is true.[7] If the police choose not to believe you, there is nothing further you can do legally to have the crime recognised by society or to have the man punished in any way. Even if the police do believe you the whole legal process is very harrowing. In no crime is it as bad as in the crime of rape. As a witness, your character is put on trial and you will be accused in court of lying. In 1976 at the Old Bailey in London, Judge Sutcliffe said in a summing up at a rape trial: 'It is well known that women in particular and small boys are liable to be untruthful and invent stories.' This is just one example of the prejudice against women in the courts. This kind of prejudice held by men, works in favour of men who rape and against women who are raped.

The greatest myth of all is the one which tells us that rape is an aberration removed from the ways in which men relate to women emotionally, sexually and physically. Our experiences over the past eight years have shown that rape is the extreme and logical conclusion of this relationship.

Why these myths exist

These myths serve the purpose of dividing and deceiving women, disguising the real level of male violence and its significance to all of us. The existence of rape is fundamental to the power structure which exists between men and women. That there are some 'rapists' about, means we must look to 'normal' men for protection – and protectors have a great deal of power to set rules of conduct for those they protect. The illusion must however be maintained that normal men are not rapists, that we can trust them to protect us – otherwise there is no reason to obey their rules. It also allows men who consider themselves to be normal to disassociate themselves from responsibility. So the vast majority of rapes that occur are defused – not seen as 'real rape' because she asked for it, enjoyed it, said no but meant yes, or even made up the whole thing.

Those crimes which are universally recognised as outrageous are defined more by the woman's character than by the crime itself. Tabloid headlines refer to women in the roles men accord us – 'young wife', 'mother of two', 'grandmother', and so on. Did you ever see an angry headline about a lesbian being raped? Peter Sutcliffe's crimes in 1975–80 only became truly shocking when he moved on from 'just raping prostitutes' to attacking 'nice girls' too. The rules imposed on our behaviour as women allow men to shift the responsibility for rape on to us wherever possible, so that most of the men who rape are seen as victims of our malicious allegations, carelessness or stupidity. There is no other crime in which so much effort is expended to make the 'victim' appear responsible – imagine the character or financial background of a robbery victim being questioned in court, for instance.

When we see the ways in which women are discredited in court, the rules by which we must abide to be afforded the protection of the law are obvious. Only if we are 'good women', 'nice girls' as defined by men, is rape taken seriously. If you are a 'young wife' it is serious – unless of course you have had sexual relationships with other men than your husband, in which case you have stepped outside the limits of this role. Similarly, a young girl who is a virgin is accorded protection but not if she has 'slept around'.

This does not make sense if rape is a crime committed against women and defined by the way we experience it. But it is not. The rape laws were originally connected to property – the seizing or devaluing of another man's property – and although less explicit today this concept is still at the root of legal practice and society's attitudes. A 'virgin' is her father's property, a wife her husband's, but only while she allows them exclusive rights do they and society give her protection.

As a prostitute, you are seen as available to and therefore the property of all men, so rape will not be recognised at all. Women who have no clear role in relation to men have no protection. As a lesbian you are seen as 'sick' – probably in need of a 'good fuck' to cure you, or bring you back into line.[8] As a single woman not having a sexual relationship with a man, you are seen as lacking, maybe frigid, too. In both these instances rape can be and is interpreted as a benefit, not a crime.

Even if your sexual relationships are not 'questionable' in any way, but you have broken any of the endless rules which restrict and control us – wearing the wrong clothes, acting as if you were free to go out as you please, and so on – it is you who will be punished, not the rapist. By not believing you, making sure you have as horrific a time as possible in court, and acquitting the man who raped you of any crime, society will make it very clear that you will get no protection if you do not obey the rules. But because the rules are so complex and contradictory, you can hardly help breaking at least one – therefore most of us become 'bad women', responsible for whatever is done to us. Our experience is thus invalidated, and the level of recognised 'real' rape kept down.

Once we see that rape is not an abnormal act, but part of the way men – not just strangers or maniacs but fathers, uncles, husbands, boyfriends, friends and professionals – treat us as women, we realise that we cannot make a distinction between 'normal men' and rapists. The silence around rape and the myths that obscure the reality have prevented women from realising that rapists are not recognisable as such. While men may choose not to commit rape, they are all capable of it and know this. When women know this too, we can stop relying on men for protection, start being angry and begin to find our own strength. In short, without this network of myths, society as we know it could not function as it does.

2
Reactions to Rape and Sexual Assault

There is no right or wrong way to react to sexual violence. You may wonder if you should or should not be feeling a certain way, how long you should feel it for or whether you shouldn't be 'over it' by now. Whatever you *do* feel is valid and right for you; each woman responds in her own way. If you can talk about your feelings with other women, it helps to understand where they come from and in this way regain control over your life.

Rape is an act which is totally controlled by the man. During rape a woman's right to be self-powered and sexually self-determined is completely denied. Our sexuality is fundamental to our sense of ourselves and such a violation takes away the control we expect to have over our bodies and our lives. Talking about what happened, affirming the reality of what you experienced and the validity of what you feel, helps to take back that control.

Everyone has ideas about what rape is – who does it, to whom and why – and women who have been raped will be affected by whatever preconceptions they themselves have held about rape as well as by the attitudes of others they come into contact with. Friends, lovers, husbands, doctors and others often project their own version of events on to yours, distorted either to fit into their theories or to protect themselves from the reality, and thereby further remove a woman's control by denying her experience.

The myths mentioned in the last chapter play a powerful part in defining rape, and none of us is immune from their influence. To understand where many of our feelings come from – guilt, self-blame, and so on – we need to look more closely at these myths and the ways they set traps for us. We will mention some common reactions

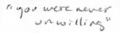

separately, later in this chapter, and hope that they will appear in a clearer perspective.

If you have always thought of rape in terms of strangers in the street, and a friend rapes you in your own home, it may be hard initially even to recognise what happened as rape, a serious crime. If you have always thought that rape happened to other women, who must have asked for it in some way, you may start assuming responsibility yourself for the rape and searching your behaviour for the provocative element – the way in which you 'broke the rules' that restrict our lives and therefore 'caused' him to rape you. Women often latch on to some commonplace action – 'I accepted a lift from him'; 'I had a drink with him'; 'I refused to have a drink with him'; 'I invited him in for coffee', and so on, and find a way like this to take the blame. But since when was inviting a man in for coffee, hitch-hiking, or having a drink an invitation to rape? It is extraordinary the lengths to which we go to blame ourselves for perfectly normal behaviour rather than blame the man for his violent and criminal act – an act which he *chooses* to commit. In no circumstances does he *have* to rape. It becomes understandable only when we look at the complex set of rules for women's behaviour that allow men to escape their responsibility in this way.

This set of rules involves so many contradictions that in society's eyes we can never win. Women are encouraged, particularly when young, to dress attractively, wear make-up, attend to our hair and in hundreds of ways and on millions of magazine pages, to do our best to 'attract a man'. Yet when we are raped we are blamed for being 'provocative' – dressed in the very same clothes, make-up and haircut – and told we were asking for it. If we do not trust men we are seen as man-haters, aggressive, unfeminine, even sick – yet when we do trust enough to accept lifts or drinks, again we 'deserve to be raped'. No wonder we often feel confused.

We are supposed to dress to please and attract but only to a certain point (an indefinable or non-existent one) after which men are no longer to be held responsible for their actions. We are supposed to be able to tell the 'goodies' whom we can trust from the 'baddies' whom we can't. But how? When the truth about rape is known – that women and girls of all ages, classes, races and appearances are raped by men who have been friends, lovers or acquaintances as well as strangers – we can see that rape is a result of the way men see and relate to women normally. It happens to us because we are women, not because of our individual age, appearance, manner of dress, behaviour or sexual desirability. (In any case who is deciding whether or not we fit the bill for being sexually desirable? On whose terms are we being judged?)

Such is the power of the male ego that men often speak of raping a woman as 'doing her a favour'. And so deeply are we all affected by the warped (male) sexuality which pervades our society that women sometimes deem themselves 'unworthy' of being raped (and therefore safe) by virtue of their age or physical appearance.

Men have enormous power in defining perceptions – of rape and of sexuality, both female and male. Who can deny the power of someone who can say 'What she really needs is a good . . .' and in a tone of voice that is far from friendly or admiring, but that is nothing short of contemptuous.

The common perception of rape bears little relation to the reality. Rape is not merely 'sexual intercourse' – rape is force, rape is fear, rape is violence. Yet it is no coincidence that it is men who come up with this definition and thus cloud our perception of the reality. No coincidence that male defence counsel in rape trials will casually slip in the phrase 'making love' when describing rape to a woman being cross-examined: 'So then he made love to you again, did he?'

Men benefit from these misconceptions; and we can expect little support from them in exposing these myths for what they are. Thus it is for women to speak out about the reality of rape and to refuse to go on accepting not only the after-effects of, but also the blame for, what is done to us. By talking with other women about our experiences, we validate our own reality and release ourselves from the traps which male myths set for us. Rape is not only an individual experience, but part of a much larger pattern of the relationship between the sexes. Holding on to what has happened as an isolated act can lock you into the circle of self-blame – variations on 'What did I do? What is it about me?' – and deny you the support and reassurance to be gained from other women. If it were somehow possible to put every woman or girl who has been raped into contact with every other woman or girl, to hear our own thoughts, feelings, reactions mirrored to an unbelievable degree of accuracy, then we would all emerge into the daylight with a collective strength and anger truly intimidating in its proportions.

As it is, many women are left fighting on their own, dealing not only with physical effects, but also surrounded by myths and prejudices that deny their reality; fighting the guilt, the fear, the shame, the physical repulsion, and at some point, the anger.

Our reactions

We do not intend to prescribe how women should react to being raped. We simply describe what we know from our own experiences and from those of the women who have contacted the London Rape Crisis Centre. Each woman has her own individual way of coping with rape depending on her circumstances. By describing some of the reactions to being raped we hope to give women strength to recognise they are not going mad, and to cope with some of their feelings – in short, to enable you to take control by understanding some of the apparently uncontrollable feelings you might have.

Shock

You are likely to suffer some degree of shock after being raped. This may take various forms, from being completely calm and unemotional to shaking, crying or laughing hysterically, twitching, inability to think, and so on. It may occur immediately or some time later. If you have injuries you should get medical treatment. Otherwise it is nothing to worry about. It is helpful to have a woman friend with you for support; it is important to keep warm. (See Chapter 6, p. 67 for further details.)

Loss of control

When a man rapes you he is using his power as a man to frighten and degrade. He is telling you that your wishes and feelings are not important; that you are there for his use and nothing else. This complete disregard for your wishes is made very clear in this act of violence against you. The feeling of not having what you want taken into consideration stays with you afterwards (as well as the violence). Moreover, you are made to feel responsible for the fact that he has done this to you.

Rape throws our powerlessness sharply into focus. Most women, after being raped, are left with an inability to make decisions because we discover our decisions count for nothing. That is why it is such a traumatic act. We are reminded of our powerlessness in many different ways by men – every day. When we are raped, it is made so clear that we cannot very easily throw off the knowledge that what we want and what we say are irrelevant.

Carrying on 'as normal'

Many women, contrary to popular mythology, carry on living 'as normal' after being raped. Control over your sexuality, your actions and your life are taken away from you when you are raped. It is not surprising, therefore, that you might decide to hang on to what control you can after such an experience. You may refuse to let it affect you, carry on going to work, caring for your children, not telling anyone about it, burying it deep inside. But it is difficult to ignore rape. The reminders are numerous – jokes, newspaper articles, advertising, conversations at work, everyday sexual harassment . . . the list is endless. At some point, too, you are likely to feel very angry – and very vulnerable. It is important to take some time for yourself, to be cared for, not to expect too much of yourself.

Nightmares

Many women have nightmares after being raped. These can take the form of specific and detailed images of the rape itself – or they can be vague terrifying shapes or feelings. They can make you afraid to go to sleep – sapping your strength. For many of us such nightmares are reminders of sexual assaults we experienced as children and had managed to forget. It is important to try to deal with these nightmares somehow. One way to do it is to talk about both the nightmares and the feelings they are bringing up for you, and the details of the rape itself with someone you trust. By talking about them, you share the burden of what is in your head, and you can also pick the dreams to pieces and in doing so control them. This does not necessarily mean that the nightmares will go away. It does, however, mean that you recognise them when they come and will hopefully be able to wake someone up and ask for support at the time, rather than suffering many sleepless nights.

Fear

One of the most common beliefs about rape, amongst men particularly, is that rape of one able-bodied woman by one bigger, stronger, able-bodied man without a weapon such as a gun, knife, or broken bottle to hand is not physically possible. You are assumed to be able to deliver the proverbial well-placed kick, thereby temporarily disabling your assailant, after which you run for your life and escape. This seemingly easy escape route has one huge and largely unrecognised flaw – unrecognised that is by all save the women who have been in such a situation – fear. It can literally freeze you to the spot on which you stand. Fear of being beaten (or beaten still more), fear of mutilation, fear for your life. Countless women, in describing the attack, have said: 'I honestly thought I was not going to get out of it alive.'

Such totally paralysing terror can very easily prevent you from screaming, and can most certainly scotch any ideas about kicks, well placed or otherwise. It is understandable that the terror we are made to feel when being raped will not automatically disappear afterwards.

It must also be recognised that, as women, we are brought up on a diet of fear from childhood. We are taught as little girls to be afraid of strangers, bogeymen, monsters (all invariably male). That fear is reinforced in books, films, stories – all usually portraying terrible things happening to women at the hands of monstrous (mad) men. Our fear is fed also by publicity about individual men who rape and/or murder large numbers of women. The most recent example of this is the case of the man who murdered 13 women in the North of England. While he was at large we were treated to sinister recordings of what was apparently his voice, detailed descriptions of his 'victims' and numerous exhortations to make sure we were 'safe'. He became a folk hero. What was ignored while he was at large, was the other rapes and murders carried out by different men at the same time. Somehow he became the embodiment of our fears – and of course he supposedly had little in common with other 'normal' men. When faced with a 'rapist' it is not surprising that images of men such as the 'ripper' come into our minds, and the atrocities he committed also come into our minds. Is it any wonder that we freeze?

Fear can paralyse you after being raped. It can appear to be beyond your control. You may well find it impossible to go into a place or situation in any way resembling the one in which you were raped. It could be anywhere – a car, a telephone box, an underground walkway, a certain street or area, a room in your own home. There are also other things which may bring the fear back in a flash – certain words or phrases, films, books, a particular kind of car engine, a smell . . . all these become terrorisers in their own right. You may feel scared of going out, or the opposite.

It is possible to fight this fear, to function despite it. You will probably have done so before being raped. The illusion that we are safe from rape because we are not a 'certain type of woman' or because we don't live in a 'certain type of area' often enables us to function normally. Being raped shatters these illusions. By recognising the reality we can protect ourselves from being raped to a certain extent in a much more honest and effective way (see Chapter 9).

Shame

The fact that very few of us have bodies which conform to the images that 'fashion' portrays, makes us unhappy with them anyway. Having them violently abused confirms our feelings that they are not worthy of respect. It is a telling fact that so many women feel so dreadfully ashamed of the crime that was committed against them – a reversal of the situation where you would normally feel ashamed. However, it is a pointer towards just how deeply the act of rape can touch and affect our innermost selves and a reflection of the powerful myths that allow and encourage women to feel responsible for the crime.

Most women feel physically dirty and spend a lot of time washing over and over again in order to try to feel clean. It is important to know that such behaviour and feelings are quite usual and are simply a manifestation of the fact that a man has used your body sexually without your consent. Having a VD check-up and knowing that you have not contracted an infection from the man who raped you, or having such an infection treated can help you feel cleaner, as can realising that it was nothing in you personally that made him rape you – you were raped because you were a woman and for no other reason, whatever he or anyone else says.

Feeling dirty can extend to your home; especially if you were attacked there, because everything touched by the rapist, or reminding you of the attack, often feels contaminated and violated. Cleaning your home can be a kind of 'exorcism' – washing away your feelings of guilt and dirt. This cleaning may appear to be out of control – you may not be able to stop it. As with washing your body a lot, as you begin to feel better about yourself you will regain control over this area of your life along with others. Equally, not cleaning your home at all is understandable. You may feel that neither you nor your home is worth cleaning.

Guilt

As we said earlier, almost every woman who is raped feels guilty to some extent for what has happened. You can always think of something you could have done to stop it happening. 'If only I had locked the door'; 'if only I had not accepted the lift'; 'if only I had screamed more loudly, or not screamed at all' – the list of 'if onlys' is endless. That feeling of guilt is exacerbated by men and their institutions with which you will come into contact after you have been raped.

Both the police and legal system and the medical profession will either tell you that you are lying or that it was your fault. Friends and family can imply the same with questions like 'Why didn't you lock your door?'; 'Why did you accept the lift?'; 'Why did you talk to him?', ad nauseam. It is not therefore surprising that you will firmly believe yourself to be as guilty (if not more so) than the man who raped you.

Powerlessness

As well as feeling guilty about the rape many women also feel completely powerless to make decisions. It is as though you feel so bad and worthless having brought such a terrible thing upon yourself that any decision you might make is totally invalid – or even evil. Friends and family are not always helpful in this as they are often anxious to make decisions for you anyway. It is important for you to learn to make decisions again and realise that they are good and valid. Once you stop feeling responsible for what has happened to you, and recognise where the blame lies, you might see that you probably had very few choices on which to decide anyway. As women we have very few choices in our interactions with men. However, we can and do make positive decisions about our own lives and we have a right to do this.

Immediately after being raped there are decisions you will have to make, the consequences of which will last for a long time afterwards. The first is whether or not to report the crime to the police. Friends and family can help with this one by obtaining information for you (if you can't do it yourself) on what you are getting involved in if you do report (see p. 41). It is important that you weigh what you will go through at the hands of the police and legal system against how you will feel if you get no recognition from society for the crime that has been committed against you. You are the only one who will have to live with the consequences of that decision and no one else should try to make it for you.

Physical repulsion

You may well feel unable to touch anyone else, or have anyone else touch you. Having had your body violated sexually you may, quite rightly, want to protect it from further abuse. If you report to the police you will have to endure a medical examination usually performed by a male police surgeon who is interested not in your welfare, but in collecting forensic evidence. Very soon after being raped, therefore, you will have been touched again, not as a person but as an object. This is extremely distressing and will probably leave you with either the feeling that your body is worthless and can be abused by anyone or the feeling that you want to protect it from further abuse – or a mixture of both.

If you have children you may find you do not want to cuddle them, or let them touch you. The same applies to other relatives and friends. As far as lovers are concerned, especially men, this can be a real problem. Men find it difficult to accept when you do not want any sexual contact with them. You may well be told that the way to 'get over' the rape is to have a good sexual experience. You may also feel that you want to be cuddled by a man – and of course he may interpret this as a desire for sexual contact. It is very difficult in this situation to explain what you do want – so you may develop what the experts call 'vaginismus' – a tightening of the vaginal muscles when a man attempts to penetrate you. It is in fact really important that you are able to take some control over your sexual contact with a man, after being raped. If you can do this and recognise it as a good and healthy development then you will eventually feel better about yourself and your choices. It is essential that you take some control over as many areas of your life as possible, and sexual control is fundamental. If your lover is a woman, you may also have difficulties about sexual contact. Women do have much more understanding about the importance of control and about the implications of being raped than men; however, wanting a hug or a cuddle one minute and not wanting one the next is very confusing for both your lover and yourself, and it is important that your lover recognises your confusion and that you don't feel responsible for hers. This is something that is quite positive for many of us. Women on the whole are taught from childhood to be loving, physically acceptable and accepting. It is good to change this and to decide with whom and when you have sexual contact. After being raped it may seem that you are going 'overboard' with such control, but it is probably more true that what you are doing is, for the first time, exercising *some* control.

You may feel that the way to control your sexuality and get back at men in the same way that they hurt you is to 'sleep around' – picking up men and dropping them, showing that you do not care about them. You may try to treat them as unfeelingly and hatefully as they have treated you. There is a problem with this because we as women are not in a position to violate men in the same way that they violate us. We cannot rape, and even sexually assaulting a man will not hurt him in the same way that he has hurt you. This is because you will not have the backing of society and its male-run institutions to make him feel humiliated and afraid. Also being a 'bad' woman will probably make you feel guilty and even worse about yourself.

It may also occur to you that the way to 'recover' from being raped, not to be beaten, is to show yourself and the world that your ability to relate to men sexually has not been 'damaged'. However, it is a man who has violated your sexuality by raping you, and rape is part and parcel of the way in which we are normally treated by men in this society. It is therefore unlikely that you will feel any better or more in control of your sexuality by having sexual intercourse with lots of men. A much better way to get control is to think about yourself, who you want to relate to sexually, when you want to do this (if ever), where and how. By exercising this kind of control you are likely to be much stronger and happier.

Another reason for 'sleeping around' is that many women, after being raped, feel completely worthless and useless. You may feel that your body is not worth protecting, that men should be free to use someone as 'bad' as you as much as they please. This is, in effect, what they are telling you when they rape you. It may feel as though a particular man has raped you for a particular reason, or that you have 'attracted' the rape by virtue of some quality that you do or do not possess. However, men rape women because we are *women* – we, individually, have no responsibility for that. Even if you were being punished personally for something by a man you know, the fact that he chose rape rather than anything else to punish you takes his action out of the realms of personal relationships and into the reality of male–female power relationships. In this way you bear no responsibility for the crime.

Depression

Although depression is a common reaction to being raped it often goes unrecognised; the early waking, the general lack of feelings or the crushing dull moods which are recognisable characteristics of depression can be interspersed with times of feeling far more 'up' and 'normal'. Like the feeling of physical repulsion we mentioned earlier, there is often no telling when the moods of despair will come or for how long they will stay, or when they will disappear once and for all.

Most doctors, upon making the diagnosis of depression, will prescribe anti-depressant drugs. While these drugs may temporarily serve to lighten your mood and may therefore be useful when your depression has reached such depths that no one is able to communicate with you, they are prescribing to relieve the symptom and not the cause of the depression. The discovery that those methods by which we are taught to protect ourselves do not work; the discovery of the injustice with which we are treated by men; the betrayal of your trust of someone else; all these and the many other realities you face after being raped are quite sufficient to depress you.

Recognising depression as a specific reaction is the first step in dealing with it – to be able to group together all those amorphous feelings of unease and say to yourself: 'This is depression and I am feeling depressed for a good reason.' Talking about how you feel with someone you trust who can understand what you are saying usually brings a sense of relief and of sharing a burden, as well as beginning to clarify why you are depressed.

Depression can sometimes be, among other things, anger turned inwards. Once you recognise that the man who raped you *chose* to do so, and you begin to feel justifiably angry with him, you gain more strength and feel more able to fight back.

Anger

Anger can be the culmination of many different feelings; frustration at your inability to get back at the man who raped you, the enforced realisation of your own powerlessness, outrage at the effect the assault has had on you, impatience with the responses you have received from other people, indignation that any man can believe he has the right to rape you, anger at yourself for not having got yourself out of the situation. Anger is a positive and very natural reaction to such an outrageous act as rape. Shifting the blame from yourself to the man who chose to commit the crime encourages your anger to become focused on him rather than on you.

Anger at men you know (be they boyfriend, lover, brother, father or friend) is not unjustified, although they may believe it is. When a particular man rapes you it throws into focus many of the ways in which all men oppress us, and you are right to be angry about that. Maybe none of the men you know has raped you, but when you are raped you realise that in fact any one of them might have done so if they chose, especially if you *were* raped by a friend, acquaintance or relative.

Anger at rape is justified, on a personal level and on the more general level; the anger of all women towards all men that they should not only be able to choose to rape, but that so often they expect us to take the blame for it.

Reactions of family and friends

If a member of your family or a friend is raped or sexually assaulted, you will not remain unaffected. The way you react to what has happened is crucial to a woman's well-being. Women are, at the best of times, very aware of how other people are reacting to them. We are trained from an early age to be attractive – to see ourselves mirrored in other people's (especially men's) eyes. Other people's approval is very important to us. After being raped, a woman's self-esteem is very low and she will be especially sensitive to how you are treating her. This section will describe some of the things you will probably feel if a friend or relative tells you she has been raped. It will also provide some pointers for you on how to deal with how you feel in a way which is most helpful to the woman.

It is important first, to make it clear that you *believe* what the woman tells you. Secondly, that you explore your own feelings and understand them before you try to start understanding how she feels. She will have enough to cope with without having to worry about what you are feeling. Below are some of the reactions you may have.

Concerned 'taking over'

One of the most common reactions of those closest to a woman who has been raped is to want to take over, to spare her the pain of any decisions or action. While such motives are understandable, they can continue to make a woman feel that events are entirely out of her control. Rape takes away our control, both during and after the actual assault. It is therefore crucial that the woman be allowed to begin the process of regaining that control. The way to ensure that this happens is not by making decisions on her behalf (even if it appears that she is not capable of making the decision), but to provide her with information and allow her time to make her own decisions.

One of the most important decisions a woman will have to make after being raped is whether or not to report the crime to the police. Relatives and friends, on hearing of the rape, often either press a woman to report or actually take the matter out of her hands and phone the police for her. Apart from reinforcing her helplessness, this action will embroil a woman in a very painful and lengthy legal process. It is much more helpful in this situation to find out what the process involves, telling her about it and talking with her about whether or not *she wants* to report, leaving the decision up to her. She, not you, will have to live through the consequences of that decision. If you have a preconceived idea about what the woman should do, it is better to leave it to someone else to speak with her about it. It will not do, for example, for a woman to be emotionally blackmailed into thinking that she must report, in order to prevent the man from raping someone else. It is not her responsibility to stop the man doing what he alone chooses to do – nor is it her fault that the legal system is so unsympathetic to women who have been raped.

Anger

Most people have an immediate sense of anger towards the rapist for what he has done to their friend. This anger is perfectly understandable, but, while you should let the woman know that you believe her and are angry at the rapist (not her), it is important not to let it override any decisions she might want to make. Men, especially, are prone to a protective anger expressed, for example, in the sentiment 'I'm going to kill him' – or some such threat. Saying this to a woman who has just been raped is not helpful – she will then not only feel responsible for what has happened to her and how she feels, but also for what might happen to you if you do carry out the threat.

Equally, it is not helpful to express any anger you might feel towards the woman for 'getting herself into the situation' or for 'asking for it'. No woman asks to be raped or sexually assaulted. She will be busy blaming herself for what has happened anyway, and your reinforcing that will only make her feel worse. It must be recognised that the only person responsible for rape is the man who commits the crime.

Guilt

You may feel guilty about something you may or may not have done in the time leading up to the rape. Again, you are not responsible for what has happened. If a man chooses to rape a woman it is his choice, and it is usually planned well in advance. Blaming yourself will only make the woman feel more guilty than *she* already feels by bringing that pain to you.

Helplessness

You may not know what to do next when a friend or relative tells you that she's been raped. It is probably best to look after her physically, tell her that you care for her, try not to treat her differently from before. It is most important that you respect her decisions and take your lead on what to do from her. Try and take your own feelings and distress elsewhere. She probably needs your support if she is telling you what happened. If you are a woman then there is support and information available for you from rape crisis centres, as well as for the woman who has been raped herself.

Wanting to 'make it better'

Most people, once the initial shock and trauma have worn off, want their friend or relative to be 'better' – back to 'normal'. Rape significantly changes your perception of your life and of the world you live in. You do not 'get over' such an experience. It cannot be wiped out, or forgotten. There is no time limit after which you should have 'recovered' from being raped. Each individual woman assimilates the experience into her life according to her individual circumstances. This can take from months to years.

It is important that you, as a friend or relative, do not treat a woman any differently from before. If you are doing so, you need to be clear why *you* have changed. It is important that you take responsibility for that change and not expect the woman to take it. If you feel that the woman herself has changed, then it is important that you discuss those changes with her and accept them. Sometimes changes are very positive ones.

You may feel that having a sexual relationship with you or someone else will help a woman 'recover' (or prove that she has 'recovered') from being raped. First of all, you do not 'recover' from being raped. The most important thing about being raped is the fact that it takes control of your life away. Women struggle in all kinds of ways to get that control back. One of the most important ways to do this is in her sexual contact. It is vital that she does take control in this area, and that she is not punished for doing so. Most women have very little sexual control anyway, so exercising any takes a lot of courage and should be encouraged. By sexual control we mean saying with whom, where, how and when she has sexual contact with anyone, man or woman.

Finally, it is important that women get a chance to talk to someone they feel comfortable with about the experience. If you are that person, then it is important that you listen and empathise with what she is saying. If you are a woman that should not be difficult; we all live in the same fear of rape, and can all imagine quite easily how it feels. Hearing of a friend's rape might remind you of a similar experience you might have had either as an adult or as a child. If this happens then it is important that you get support for and recognition of your feelings either from your friend or from a rape crisis centre. Your feelings might well affect how you respond to your friend, and you may become over-involved in her sense of being out of control and feel out of control yourself. If you are a man you cannot empathise wth a woman about rape. It is better that she seek support either from a woman friend or relative she feels comfortable with, or from a rape crisis centre.

3
The Law

The law on sexual offences is unfortunately no less complicated than in any other area. In this chapter we present background information that we hope will make police and court procedure (see the next two chapters) seem more understandable. We define the charges most likely to be brought and describe the most common defences used to get the man off.

The law we are describing is English law. Laws and practices in other English-speaking countries may vary, but they share most of the assumptions and many of the details of English law.

The history of the law on rape and related offences is based on protecting the property of men.

In the Middle Ages the law was preoccupied on the one hand with the preservation of virginity and the provision of legitimate heirs, and, on the other, with the protection of family interests and the succession to landed property. The penalty for rape was loss of life and member, but this savage punishment, as Bracton stressed, applied only when the victim was a virgin. The evil that the law tried to prevent was the abduction of propertied virgins who, to the detriment of family rights in their disposal, were thus compromised into marriage. The essence of the crime was theft of another man's property, and the victim's point of view was sometimes excluded to such an extent that the sexual aspect of the case might be found in the words 'swived against the will of her father'. Once the law had accepted theft as the *sine qua non* of rape it was only logical to hold that a husband is no more capable of raping his wife than an owner is of stealing his own property.[1]

Today the law on rape and sexual offences, police and court procedures still reflect this history. It is clear that their primary concern is not the protection of women and we often appear and feel incidental once the legal process itself is set in motion.

After you have reported to the police you do not have any say in what charge is made. The initial charge is decided by the police and will be based largely on your complaint, but the final conviction may well be for a crime unrecognisable as your experience. This is due to a process called 'plea-bargaining', which the lawyers for both sides commonly practise. For example, the man may plead 'not guilty' to a charge of rape but be prepared to plead 'guilty' to a charge of indecent assault, for which he will probably get a much lighter sentence. If the lawyer acting for the police, that is, on your side (the 'prosecution counsel'), thinks your case is not very strong, he may accept this, rather than push for a conviction of rape that may not be successful. You cannot stop this happening. It can be very upsetting as it belittles and denies the crime actually committed against you.

The two main Acts of Parliament covering sexual offences are the 1956 Sexual Offences Act and the 1976 Sexual Offences (Amendment) Act. There are also Acts specific to offences against children, for example, the Children and Young Persons Act 1933 and the Indecency with Children Act 1960. There is presently a committee sitting to review the law on sexual offences – the Criminal Law Revision Committee – out of whose recommendations changes in the law will be planned.[2]

Criminal law is made up of statute law (Acts of Parliament) and 'common law' (or 'case law'), which is a body of unwritten rules (for example murder and assault are not defined by statute). The meaning of statutes and the common law is interpreted by judges, from case to case. Judges in Crown Courts are bound by the interpretation of the law given by the Court of Appeal, the High Court (Divisional Court) and the House of Lords.

Unless stated otherwise, this is the law in England and Wales. Ireland, Northern Ireland and Scotland have differences both in actual law and procedures which are summarised separately.

For a woman raped abroad, information about the country's legal system can be gained from the British consular department in the country concerned, or a rape crisis centre if they have one. You will be unlikely to receive any help from legal or government sources in this country, though contacting the embassy concerned will give you the address of the consular department. Although law varies from country to country and within the British Isles, anti-women attitudes remain the same.

Charges

1. Rape

The offence of rape is legally defined in the Act of 1976 as when a man 'has unlawful' (i.e. extra-marital) 'sexual intercourse with a woman without her consent, and at that time he knows that she does not consent to the intercourse or is reckless as to whether or not she consents to it'. Rape is further defined as intercourse:

(a) by force or fear of death or serious injury to yourself or your close relatives (i.e. if you are threatened and give in);

(b) by fraud, for example where a woman consents believing the man to be performing a medical operation, or where the man is impersonating the woman's husband (Sexual Offences Act 1956);

(c) when the woman is asleep, unconscious, drugged, or so severely mentally handicapped,[3] or so young (under 16) as to be unable to understand the nature of the act and so not be in a position to consent or resist.

For a charge of rape to be brought, there must have been some penetration, either penis–vagina or penis–labia (outer lips). Ejaculation need not have taken place. The courts usually require evidence of both penetration and force as corroboration (see below) – a woman's word is not usually enough. Where a man has committed other offences – for example, grievous bodily harm, actual bodily harm, attempted murder, abduction (kidnapping) – he will usually only be charged with rape and evidence of the other offences (cuts, bruises, broken bones etc.) will be used to support that charge. If there is no evidence of struggle – say, where a woman judged the best way of getting away with as little physical injury as possible was to do as the man told her – it is usually difficult to get a charge brought. If penetration cannot be proved (by the medical examination), the charge may be attempted rape or indecent assault (see below).

A rape offence, as defined in the 1976 Act, includes attempted rape, aiding, abetting, counselling and procuring rape, and incitement to rape. All these crimes are related to rape and the law on rape – for example, regarding anonymity and past sexual history – is applicable to them too.

Rape cases are tried only in Crown Courts, but all criminal cases have to start in Magistrates' Courts (see Chapter 5, Committal). The maximum sentence is life imprisonment, the average sentence 2–4 years. In 1980[4] only four men received life imprisonment (out of 421 found guilty of rape in England and Wales). Nineteen percent of the men convicted were not sentenced to immediate imprisonment and, of the remainder, over 50 percent received sentences of three years or under (see Table 1).

Rape in marriage   Women can be and are raped by their husbands, but in the UK a husband cannot be charged with the rape of the woman he is married to unless they are *legally* separated or divorced, or unless the woman has been granted an injunction against her husband for non-molestation and non-interference, or he has undertaken not to molest her, and *it is in force at the time of the rape.* These legal actions remove the obligation placed on a woman by marriage always to consent to sexual intercourse with her husband. If there was no legal separation, undertaking or injunction, the charge could be actual bodily harm or grievous bodily harm where physical force was used. If a husband helps others rape the woman he's married to, he could be charged with conspiracy, aiding or abetting, or incitement, or procuring rape, or all or some of these. As can be seen, women who are married are afforded little protection in law from their husbands. The assumption is made that having consented once, you have consented forever, no matter how unreasonable that assumption is.

Boys under 14   A boy under 14 cannot be found guilty of rape (except in Scotland), but can be charged with aiding and abetting, or with indecent assault.

2. Attempted rape

This charge may be brought when there is insufficient evidence of penetration, but clear evidence that that was what the man intended. It is often clear to *us* that a man tried to rape us – it is rarely clear to the police and courts. It is not often brought as a charge. Attempted rape cases go through Magistrates' Courts and Crown Courts. The maximum sentence is seven years' imprisonment, the average sentence 18 months.

3. Indecent assault

The 1956 Act makes indecent assault on a woman or girl an offence, but gives no clear definition of what it is. From case law we know it includes: forced penetration of mouth by the penis, forced penetration of anus or vagina by an object (for example, stick, bottle or hand), and touching of breasts or bottom or genital area without a woman's consent. A woman under the age of 16 cannot consent to any of these acts – for women over 16, consent is an issue.

That penetration other than penis–vagina is not given weight as a serious offence, can be seen by the maximum sentences for indecent assault and by the fact that cases can be tried either in Magistrates' or Crown Courts. The maximum sentence is two years' imprisonment where the woman is over 13, and five years imprisonment where the woman is under 13. (By way of comparison, the maximum sentence for indecent assault on a man is ten years.) In 1980,[5] of the 2423 men found guilty of indecent assault on a woman, only 359 were sentenced to immediate imprisonment (14.8 percent). Of those sentenced at Crown Court (246 men), only 15 percent got sentences longer than two years, the most common prison sentence being 6–18 months. The total number of offences of indecent assault on a woman recorded by the police in that year was 11,498 – in 1067 cases the police chose to caution the offender rather than to prosecute at all.

4. Buggery

Buggery is penetration, forced or not, of the anus by the penis. Anal penetration is legal only between two consenting adult men (over 21) in private. A woman cannot therefore consent to buggery and can be charged as well if it is suggested that she did. Although women are not usually charged, consent is often an issue throughout the legal process. As with rape, penetration can be to any degree, and ejaculation need not take place.

Buggery cases go through Magistrates' to Crown Courts. The maximum sentence is life imprisonment.

5. Attempted buggery

This may be charged where penetration cannot be proved. The maximum punishment is ten years' imprisonment. There is also an offence called 'assault with intent to commit buggery', the maximum sentence for which is ten years' imprisonment.

6. Indecent exposure

This is the charge brought when a man exposes his penis to a woman, commonly known as 'flashing'. It comes under the Vagrancy Acts of 1824 and therefore does not constitute a sexual offence in law. Indecent exposure cases are tried in a Magistrates' Court. The maximum sentence is three months imprisonment or a £200 fine; on second conviction the sentence can go up to one year.

7. Other related charges

Usually all the crimes committed when rape occurs, including abduction (kidnapping), administering of drugs, burglary, grievous bodily harm, actual bodily harm and attempted murder, are not charged. They are used as evidence in court that you were raped, thus denying that crimes other than rape have been committed. That separate crimes are not charged and acknowledged demonstrates the lack of seriousness with which rape as a crime in itself is viewed. Rape has a low conviction rate, and when men are acquitted, as they often are, they are then let off the other crimes they have committed. This could be seen as a positive encouragement to men who are intent on committing crimes to rape women.

8. Incest

Sexual intercourse between father and daughter, brother and sister, grandfather and grand-daughter, son and mother is illegal. If you are raped by your father, brother, grandfather or son, the charge brought will be incest, not rape. If the woman is under the age of 16 she cannot in law consent, and cannot therefore be charged. Over the age of 16, a woman can be charged too if she consented. This threat is often used to stop women reporting, though convictions against women are rare and a Home Office study found no women imprisoned for this offence in the period looked at.[6]

Where sexual acts other than intercourse have taken place, charges can be brought as described elsewhere in this chapter; for example, a father can be charged with indecent assault, gross indecency with a girl under 14, buggery and so on. Uncles, stepfathers, adoptive and foster fathers, nephews and cousins cannot be charged with incest but can be charged with all other sexual offences including rape. The law on incest is therefore primarily concerned with the prevention of congenital abnormalities, and not with the protection of women and girls.

Incest cases go through Magistrates' Courts to Crown Courts. The maximum sentence is life imprisonment if the girl is under 13 years. If she is over 13 it is only seven years, compared with life if the charge is rape. The view that women contribute to the crime of incest and the myth of the blameless man, are clearly entrenched in and reinforced by the law. In 1980[7] there were 312 offences of incest recorded by the police and 141 men convicted. Ninety-seven were sentenced to immediate imprisonment, the most common prison sentences being between two and four years.

9. Attempted incest
This charge is brought when there is insufficient evidence of penetration, but clear evidence that that was what the man intended. It applies to the same family members and ages as incest above.

Cases go through Magistrates' Courts to Crown Courts. The maximum sentence is seven years if the girl is under 13, two years if she is over 13.

10. Unlawful sexual intercourse with young women
Sexual intercourse with a girl under 16 years of age is illegal. Although she cannot in law consent, in practice consent is often an issue throughout the legal process. This charge is often brought when a young woman has in fact been raped, as force does not have to be

proved. A prosecution can only be brought up to 12 months from when the offence was committed, where the girl is aged between 13 and 16 years.

Unlawful sexual intercourse (USI) with a girl aged under 13 is triable in Crown Court only. If the girl is between 13 and 16 it can be tried in either the Magistrates' Court or the Crown Court. There are two offences: sexual intercourse with a girl under 13, for which the maximum sentence is life imprisonment, and sexual intercourse with a girl under 16, for which the maximum sentence is two years (compared with a maximum sentence of life if the charge of rape is brought). Many cases never reach court – in 1976–77 the police cautioned twice as many adults as they prosecuted, and ten times as many juveniles. Those who are prosecuted and convicted are frequently given non-custodial sentences, though the younger the girl (usually under 12) and the older the offender, the more likely a prison sentence becomes.

In 1980,[8] 102 men were found guilty of USI with a girl under 13 and a further 54 cautioned, out of 254 offences recorded by the police. Forty-five men received immediate prison sentences. In the same year, there were 3109 offences of USI with a girl under 16 recorded by the police. 1340 offenders received only a caution, 565 more were found guilty in court and 76 of these sentenced to immediate imprisonment.

11. Gross indecency

The Indecency with Children Act 1960 makes it an offence for a person to commit an act of gross indecency with or towards a child under 14, or to incite a child under that age to such an act with him. This includes a man asking a girl to touch his genitals or forcing her to do so – whether or not she touches him is irrelevant.

Gross indecency cases can be dealt with at Magistrates' Court or Crown Court. The maximum penalty is two years' imprisonment at Crown Court, six months at Magistrates' Court.

In 1980,[9] 260 men were found guilty of gross indecency with a child. Thirty-five received immediate prison sentences.

Defences

This is a legal term (see p. 131 for a full glossary of legal terms and their meanings) meaning the arguments – or excuses if you like – put forward by a man accused of rape. Every man denying a sexual offence will have a defence, decided upon with his solicitor or barrister, on which his whole argument in court will be based.

Consent

This is the defence most commonly used because it is the most successful in obtaining an acquittal. In essence it means that the man (or men) is agreeing that sexual intercourse did take place with you, but claims it was not against your will; in other words you agreed to everything that happened. It is also the hardest defence to refute, since it comes down to your word against the man's: he is saying you did agree, you are saying you did not – the jury must decide who is telling the truth. Consent defences are the most nerve-wracking for women to face, since the defence will depend on exploiting myths about women and rape.

The defence lawyer will try to discredit you, aiming to get the jury to doubt your word, knowing the judge will direct the jury that unless they are sure the man is guilty they must not convict. The defence has only to introduce that element of doubt, whereas the prosecution (your side) has to convince the jury beyond all doubt that the man is guilty. You are put in the position of feeling it is you that is on trial, since it must be proved that you didn't consent.

In 1975 there was a case in England which produced what became known as the *Morgan* ruling: a man should be acquitted of rape if he *honestly believed* that the woman consented, *no matter how unreasonable his belief might have been.* [10] The Law Lords did say they felt such a defence would be a desperate one, that a jury would be able to see through it, and that it was up to the judge to point out its desperate nature. But it is a good pointer to the attitudes women face in our contact with the police and legal profession, the entrenched support for the idea that we do not know our own minds.

Other defences

These include an alibi defence, where the man argues a case of mistaken identity; claiming that he has been framed and that it did not happen; that he was either incapable of performing the act or that he did not intend to do the act or know what he was doing.

Corroboration

In present practice, *even though not required by law*,[11] it is not acceptable to take a woman's statement on its own as the basis for a charge of rape, it must be backed up by corroborative evidence. Corroborative evidence includes the forensic evidence gathered at the medical examination, photographs of injuries, torn clothing etc. Your word alone, without evidence to back up your statement, is not considered sufficient to obtain a conviction for rape. One of the reference texts of the legal profession states: 'Though corroboration of the evidence of the Prosecutrix [i.e. the woman] is not essential in law, it is, in practice, always looked for and it is the established practice to warn the jury against the danger of acting upon her uncorroborated testimony.'[12] Judges have made similar comments in their summing up speeches, for example: 'It is dangerous to convict on the uncorroborated evidence of a woman.'[13] This view is based on the incorrect belief that women make false allegations of rape. If there is no corroborative evidence the police are unlikely to take up the case.

Anonymity

In cases of rape (and other rape offences; see below), the media are not allowed to publish or broadcast information which identifies you to members of the public unless the judge gives his permission.[14] The press are not allowed to publish your name and address and are supposed to limit their descriptions of you so that you cannot be recognised. No account is taken of how you might feel reading about 'your case' in the papers; sometimes too, sufficient detail is given to identify you, without actually giving your name and address.

In court, unless you specifically request otherwise, your name and address will be read out and anyone, including the man on trial, will hear it. No account is taken of your safety and it is left up to you to ask the police officer in charge of your case that this does not happen.

If the charge is other than rape or attempted rape, you do not have any protection in law and your name, address and any description of you or your life is allowed. You can request the police not to give your name and address to the media and also that they are not read out in court, but there is no guarantee that your request will be granted, or that the press will not give a description that identifies you.

The fact that anonymity both in the media and court is not guaranteed for all sexual offences shows a lack of concern for our safety and well-being. A decision to report to the police should not necessitate our going public. We should be in control of whom we tell.

Past sexual history

The law states that no questions shall be asked about the past sexual experience of a woman who has been raped[15] unless the judge gives his permission.[16] This does not however include past sexual experience with the man or men on trial. Thus, if a man with whom you have had previous sexual relations either tries to rape you or does rape you, questioning you on this relationship in court is allowed. If you have not had any previous sexual relations with the man, then the defence counsel has to make an application to the judge when the jury are out of court, if he wishes to raise your past sexual history. He is supposed to show why he considers it relevant. Despite the law and its supposed protection for women, these applications are rarely turned down and sometimes they are not even made, the defence just goes ahead and the judge allows it.[17] The defence will use any information available to him, for example, information on your past sexual and gynaeco-logical history contained in the police surgeon's report.

A woman's past sexual and gynaecological history are irrelevant to the crimes committed. They are used in court to undermine our credibility, playing on age-old prejudices against women who step outside the roles prescribed for us by men (virgin daughter or faithful wife), and thereby forfeit our rights to protection from the law.

That so much irrelevant 'evidence' is allowed in court to discredit us as witnesses means that evidence as to the facts of the crime must be enormously strong to counteract this. As usual, the law is heavily biased towards men.

Your legal position

It often comes as something of a shock to discover that your legal status in a rape prosecution is that of a witness – and nothing more. Admittedly a very important one – chief witness for the prosecution – and without you such charges cannot be brought. Nonetheless this means you cannot have your own independent legal representation (solicitor or barrister) to act on your behalf. Although there will be both solicitor(s) and barrister acting for the prosecution, you have no part in choosing them, nor are you likely to see them until the trial begins. The police have their own solicitors, who instruct barristers of their choice.

Rape is an offence against the State (Crown). The Crown is seen as the injured party and it is they who bring the prosecution against the man. You become a witness to this crime committed against the State, and the entire legal process is out of your control. They decide whether or not they want to prosecute and if so how this will be done. You have no say in these decisions and will be unlikely to have access to anyone concerned, except the police officer in charge of your case. You will therefore be given little information as to how things are proceeding.

The full costs of the prosecution are paid for out of public funds and your expenses are paid.

Scotland

The Sexual Offences Acts 1956 and 1976 do not apply to Scotland. The Sexual Offences (Scotland) Act 1976 is not an equivalent to these Acts, but a consolidation of previous legislation.

Rape in Scotland is a common law crime (i.e. developed over the centuries by the courts, through successive cases); therefore there is no statutory definition. However the definition in *Gordon* (the modern criminal law textbook) is: 'Rape is the carnal knowledge of a female by a male person obtained by overcoming her will.')

Rape carries a maximum penalty of life imprisonment. Penetration is only of the vagina by the penis; anything else is indecent assault. It must be proved that the woman's will was overcome by the degree of violence used. If a woman takes drink or drugs freely and is raped, this is not rape in law, only indecent assault. However, if she is 'plied with drink', this is rape. Other offences which could be charged are: indecent assault (maximum two years); assault with intent to ravish (maximum two years); attempted rape (maximum two years); incest (maximum life). Boys from the age of eight upwards are deemed capable of the act of rape.

Though a woman reports initially to the police, the office of the Procurator Fiscal (there is no English equivalent) decides whether or not to prosecute, what the charge(s) should be, and can also abandon proceedings once begun. If the Procurator Fiscal decides to abandon once and for all, and tells the accused, no further proceedings can take place. Procurators Fiscal are independent of the police, and have the power to instruct them.

The woman is a witness for the prosecution. She may have contact with the Procurator Fiscal during the preparation of the prosecution case, but only after the decision has been made to proceed.

Complaints about the police should be reported to the Procurator Fiscal.

There are two stages of court, broadly similar to the English system, but called first and second 'diets' (hearings). A jury has 15 jurors.

Anonymity of women complainants is the practice, though not the law. All evidence requires corroboration under Scottish law; this can be from persons (i.e. eye-witnesses), or things (for example, torn clothing, medical evidence in rape cases).

Through a loophole in Scottish law which has existed since the Middle Ages, it *is* possible for an individual to bring a private prosecution with the Crown's consent. The most common way has always been and is now for the Crown to prosecute on behalf of the individual, but a private prosecution for rape has recently been brought in Scotland. It is not known how long this loophole will be allowed to exist, however.

Republic of Ireland

Irish law is incorporated in the 1861 Offences Against the Person Act, the Criminal Law Amendment Act 1935 and the Criminal Law (Rape) Act 1981.

Rape is defined as 'Unlawful carnal knowledge without a woman's consent'. Penetration only must be proved, not rupture of the hymen or ejaculation. Rape carries a maximum penalty of life imprisonment. Other offences which could be charged are: indecent assault (maximum ten years); attempted rape (maximum ten years); incest (maximum seven years). A boy under 15 cannot be charged with rape.

The decision to prosecute rests with the Director of Public Prosecutions. There are two stages of court: District Court (the equivalent of Magistrates' Court) and Central Criminal Court (Dublin) or Circuit Criminal Court (outside Dublin). Even if there is a guilty plea at District Court, the case will still proceed to Criminal Court, since rape is a felony (as opposed to incest, for example, which is only a misdemeanour).

Under the Criminal Law Amendment Act it is a felony to commit statutory rape on a girl under 15, with or without her consent; between 15 and 17, again with or without consent, it is a misdemeanour. It is also a misdemeanour against a woman who is mentally subnormal, when the man knows she is so.

4
The Police

'Mr Smith, you were held up at gunpoint on the corner of First and Main?'

'Yes.'

'Did you struggle with the robber?'

'No.'

'Why not?'

'He was armed.'

'Then you made a conscious decision to comply with his demands rather than resist?'

'Yes.'

'Did you scream? Cry out?'

'No. I was afraid.'

'I see. Have you ever been held up before?'

'No.'

'Have you ever *given* money away?'

'Yes, of course.'

'And you did so willingly?'

'What are you getting at?'

'Well, let's put it like this, Mr Smith. You've given money away in the past. In fact you have quite a reputation for philanthropy. How can we be sure you weren't *contriving* to have your money taken by force?'

'Listen, if I wanted. . .'

'Never mind. What time did this holdup take place?'

'About 11 pm.'

'You were out on the street at 11 pm? Doing what?'

'Just walking.'

'Just walking? You know that it's dangerous being out on the street that late at night. Weren't you aware that you could have been held up?'

'I hadn't thought about it.'

'What were you wearing?'

'Let's see – a suit. Yes, a suit.'

'An *expensive* suit?'

'Well – yes. I'm a successful lawyer, you know.'

'In other words, Mr Smith, you were walking around the streets late at night in a suit that practically advertised the fact that you might be a good target for some easy money, isn't that so? I mean, if we didn't know better, Mr Smith, we might even think that you were *asking* for this to happen, mightn't we?'[1]

Absurd as this may seem in the context of robbery, transfer the scene to rape and it is a realistic picture of the questioning women reporting rape frequently face, both at the police station and later in court.

Many women choose not to report rape to the police. In fact at least 75 percent of women who have contacted the London Rape Crisis Centre have not reported the crime.[2] Reporting is an ordeal in itself and involves you in a legal process over which you have no control. It is the police and the Director of Public Prosecutions who decide whether to take up your complaint, what charge to bring, and so on, and the process can last six months to a year. Reporting does not necessarily secure a conviction by any means, nor does a conviction necessarily mean imprisonment. However, it is the only chance you have of getting the rapist published and society's recognition that he has committed a crime for which he is responsible. Many women are clear from the start, for a variety of reasons, that they don't want the police involved. Others may not want to report, but will not feel safe, or will worry about other women's safety if they do not. Whether or not to report to the police is an extremely difficult decision – unfortunately one that must be made quickly, at a time you may feel least up to doing so. It is important that you make your own decision. Whatever it is, other people should respect it – no one should report for you or try to influence you either way.

All women have the right to know what the law is, and what

Table 1: Rape[1]

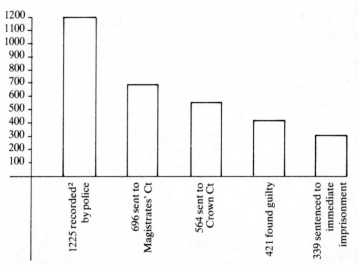

- 1225 recorded[2] by police
- 696 sent to Magistrates' Ct
- 564 sent to Crown Ct
- 421 found guilty
- 339 sentenced to immediate imprisonment

1. Figures from Home Office, *Criminal Statistics England & Wales 1980*.
2. 'Recorded' rapes are those which the police choose to investigate. They do not therefore include the total number reported to them.
The 'reported' figures are only a small percentage of actual assaults – no one knows the true incidence.

Table 2: Indecent assault on a woman[1]

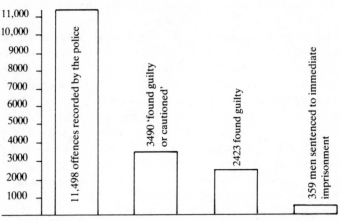

- 11,498 offences recorded by the police
- 3490 'found guilty or cautioned'
- 2423 found guilty
- 359 men sentenced to immediate imprisonment

1. Figures from Home Office, *Criminal Statistics England & Wales 1980*.

reporting rape to the police will involve them in, both at the police station and later in court. If we do report the crime committed against us, we are rarely given information that allows us to know and understand what is happening to us. That we are largely kept in do not know anything about the legal process and your position in it, you will be much 'easier to handle' in a police station, say, than if you know what should reasonably be done for you and what you can reasonably request.

Because making an *informed* decision is vital to how you live with that decision – whether it is to report or not – and its consequences, this and the next chapter deal in considerable detail with police procedure and court practice.

Reporting

When?

Contact with the police should be made as quickly as possible if it is to be made at all, since any delay lessens the chance of forensic evidence being found and also damages your credibility. Curiously, the police make the assumption that if you really have been raped, you will complain immediately. The longer you delay, the more time they assume you have had to concoct the whole story, inflict suitable injury on yourself, tear your clothes, and so on. No account seems ever to be taken by the police of a woman being in shock following a sexual assault, or of the effect on you of threats of further injury or reprisals by your assailant(s) should you tell the police.

The police will usually justify their reluctance to take up cases reported 'late' (in their terms as little as 24 hours later) by claiming there will be no forensic evidence. In fact, it is possible for sperm to be detected in the vagina even a few days after the rape.

If you do not tell the police immediately it is important that you tell someone quickly. It is the 'fact of complaint' that counts. If you tell someone other than a police officer, she or he may be called as a witness to verify early complaint, and to testify as to your state immediately after the attack. Your witness will not, however, be able to detail what you said since this would be 'hearsay' evidence, and not admissible in a court of law.

Who?

For a prosecution to go ahead you must report the crime to the police yourself. Someone else can ring the police initially and people often do without finding out if you want to get involved in the legal process, but the police will have to see you if charges are to be brought, as no prosecution can ensue without its chief witness.

It is sometimes believed that someone may make a complaint for you if you do not wish to become involved yourself in the actual prosecution process – known as 'third party reporting'. It is very rare for the police to agree to this – and if they do, there is always the risk that they may come back later and ask you to testify. It is the police's choice, not yours, whether to press charges.

Where?

The report must be made to the police station nearest to where the assault *took place*. If you go to another station first, the officers will question you, sometimes in considerable detail, but will eventually refer you to the station nearest 'the scene of the crime', where the whole process will have to be repeated with different officers. You do not have to go to a police station to make a complaint of rape; you can as easily make a statement in your own home. However, the police will invariably ask you to attend the station, rather than asking where you feel most comfortable and what you would choose. It is more intimidating to be in a police station, possibly for the first time, and it is much easier for the police officers to insist that you are alone when they question you. You may prefer to go to the police station and to be questioned alone, but your preference is not usually asked for and may not be respected. You can insist on being visited by the necessary officers at home. Or perhaps someone on your behalf can insist for you.

Your first reaction after sexual assult may be to want to wash and change your clothes. It is very important not to do this *at all* before reporting an assault to the police, though you can still report if you have. Washing will destroy valuable forensic evidence – the presence of sperm, saliva, hairs, bloodstains and so on – and the police may therefore be reluctant to take up the complaint (see Chapter 3, Corroboration).

Clothing

If you have changed your clothes since the assault, you should take with you to the station everything that you were wearing at the time of the assault, including underwear and shoes. If you are still wearing the same clothes when you go, you should take a complete change of clothing with you, since some or all of them will be removed for examination (see this chapter, p. 44, *Medical examination*). They are unlikely to be returned until after the trial.

Process

The process of reporting can take anything up to 10–12 hours, as it entails going in detail through all the facts of the incident, usually more than once, as well as a medical examination to gather corroborative evidence. In brief, then, the procedure will usually be along the following lines:

(*a*) some preliminary questioning by the officer(s) at the desk, in essence to establish the substance of the complaint and what action should be taken;

(*b*) a full statement made to CID (plain clothes) officers;

(*c*) at some point before, during or after (*b*), a medical examination.

Who should be present?

Once CID officers (detectives) are involved, you may find yourself being questioned by several different officers, usually men. In the Metropolitan Police district of London, a woman police officer (WPC) should be on hand at every station to assist in the investigation of sexual offences, but this does not necessarily happen. (The Metropolitan Police say that there will automatically be one if the woman is under 21, and over that age if she requests it.[3]) However you can insist, if you would prefer a WPC to take your statement, and it is the responsibility of the station officers concerned to find one.

Girls under 16

A WPC should automatically take the statement of a girl under 16. A parent or guardian will have to give permission for the necessary medical investigation to take place, since such an examination under that age – the age of consent – can legally constitute an indecent assault. As for the presence of others, though most police officers prefer not to have friends or relatives present during the taking of the statement with adult women, a parent, guardian or social worker should normally be present with girls under 17. Practice varies from station to station. There is no legal reason why they should not be allowed to remain throughout, so long as they do not interfere with 'the due process of the law'. (See also Chapter 7, on the sexual abuse of girls.)

Anonymity

It is also very important in these early stages to ask that your name and address be withheld in court. Normally these will be read out in open court, although the law says they must not be published. However there are many instances where women are – rightly – afraid of retaliation from the assailant or his friends or relatives. In cases of rape, it is permissible to ask (through the prosecution counsel) that your name and address not be read out in open court, but that you be allowed to write it down instead (on a piece of paper to be passed across the court). If you want to do this, such a request should be made as early and as often as possible, beginning in the police station. This only applies where the charge is rape. Where 'lesser' sexual offences are concerned you have no right to anonymity, though you can ask for your name and address to be withheld. (See also Chapter 3, p. 33.)

Medical examination

This is compulsory, even for young children. No prosecution for rape will go ahead without it (see Chapter 3, Corroboration). It will usually take place before the full statement is taken, but this will depend on the police officers concerned.

The examination can be done either by a police forensic doctor, brought in by the police, who will usually be a man (although you can request a woman), or by your own GP, if you request it. The latter has both positive and negative aspects: positive in that it will be a familiar doctor, which may help to put you at ease; negative in that many GPs do not necessarily have experience in collecting forensic evidence,[4] or else are reluctant to become involved in a case which will result in a subsequent court appearance. The examination may take place in either:

(a) the medical room in the police station where the report has been made, if there is one, or in another police station;

(b) if not, any spare room in the station (not always pleasant in atmosphere);

(c) the doctor's own surgery;

(d) a hospital.

Those present may include the doctor, a police officer (to make sure there is no malpractice), your own doctor if requested, and possibly a relative or close friend, though this may not be allowed.

The process will consist of a thorough internal and external inspection of the genital area, and the whole body. The doctor is looking for signs of physical force, inflammation, bruising or tearing. The following should also be done:

(a) swab or sample of fluid from the vagina, for traces of sperm or saliva;

(b) swab from the anus, for traces of sperm or saliva;

(c) swab from the mouth, to confirm oral penetration, and to be matched with the man's saliva;

(d) internal inspection of the vagina, for inflammation, bruising etc., and likewise the outer genitals;

(e) nail scrapings, for traces of skin, hair, grass, dirt, etc.;

(f) samples of the man's blood, if any;

(g) pubic and head hair will be combed for traces of the man's hair; they will also be cut and plucked to match against any found on the man.

(h) The doctor will look for evidence of alcohol or drug use.

Photographs of injuries may be taken immediately, or possibly a day or so later – bruising can often take 24 hours to show. If it is too early for signs of bruising, the doctor should ask you to return within 24–48 hours. If she or he does not, try and remember to raise the matter yourself with the officer in charge of your case when the bruises start to show.

This is the point at which clothing will be removed and sent to the forensic laboratory for testing, corroboration of struggle (if it is torn), and so on. It should be collected from your home by police officers if you are not already wearing it, or if you have not brought it with you.

The doctor will also assess your emotional state, take your pulse and so on; this, along with all the above, will be noted in the medical report. She or he may advise on the necessity for pregnancy and VD tests, but this is very unusual. Many women believe that they have been tested for VD and pregnancy simply by virtue of having seen the police doctor. *This is not true.* This examination is solely to collect corroborative forensic evidence. Some women also think that because they have 'seen a doctor', this means they are physically and medically 'okay'; again this is not necessarily the case. In no way should this police medical be considered a substitute for a proper check by your own doctor.

Some doctors unfortunately tend to act as amateur detectives and moralists, as well as medical practitioners. They feel it incumbent on themselves to give a personal opinion as to whether or not this woman has actually been raped. They may take the liberty therefore of asking questions about past sexual or gynaecological history: 'Are you on the pill'; 'Have you had an abortion'; 'How often do you have sex?' Such questions are irrelevant to the matter at hand. It may be necessary to establish whether you have had consensual intercourse a short time before the rape since in that case any sperm present may not necessarily be those of the rapist. Even if there are medical reasons for any such questioning, however, the responses should not be recorded in the medical report. As it is sent to the defence, such information will invariably be played on in court – however irrelevant it may be to the assault – to the detriment of you and the prosecution case.

In fact, you may be questioned in court on *any* point, however personal or intimate, and however seemingly insignificant, contained in this medical report. Such questioning, in the manner in which it is invariably done, is often felt by women as the greatest humiliation of all.

The statement

The statement will have several different uses:

    (a) as the basis of police questioning of the man when he is caught;

    (b) as the basis of the police, therefore prosecution, case;

    (c) to be sent to the man's solicitors so that the case for the defence can be prepared to counter it;

    (d) it is likely to be the only record of the assault to which a woman has access.

As a witness you can write the statement in your own words, at your own pace. However most police officers will want to write it for you since they have accepted statement 'jargon', and understand what is necessary for a prosecution. It can be disturbing to have your story 'edited' in this fashion, as it may not seem to reflect the reality of what happened. If you feel uncomfortable about this, you can insist on writing it yourself if you feel strong enough. You should also read it yourself, on completion, even if a police officer offers to do it for you. It is always best to know exactly what you are signing (see also this chapter, p. 48, *Withdrawing charges*).

It is also worth noting at this point that you can leave the station at any time, returning perhaps the following day to complete your statement. There is no law requiring witnesses to complete a statement at one sitting. If you feel too exhausted or incoherent to continue with an especially long and detailed statement, you should be allowed some rest before returning to complete it. While this is so, such a request may not always meet with a sympathetic response, the assumption presumably being that any delay might allow opportunity for embellishment or embroidering of the 'story'. Once again, this is an issue of control, as well as an example of the shaky credibility that women have when it comes to reporting sexual offences.

Copy of the statement

As stated previously, your statement to investigating police officers is likely to be the only detailed record available of what actually happened – unless, that is, you were sufficiently in command to have made notes of events immediately after the assault. Strictly speaking, you are entitled to a copy of it at any time up to the day of the trial, should you request it (though the police are not legally required to give it to you). Official opinion on this issue seems somewhat divided: 'Although there is no objection to a witness recording or making a copy of his [sic] statement for his own use, supplying him with a copy is not favoured and can be criticised in important cases.'[5] But '. . . as a witness is entitled to a copy of any statement he [sic] has made to the police there is nothing to prevent him refreshing his memory right up to the moment he enters the court. . .'[6]

While therefore there appears no legal reason why you *cannot* be given a copy, police officers, for no apparent reason, are often reluctant to give it. It seems obvious that if you are to be an effective witness for the prosecution, you *must* be given the opportunity to refresh your memory, some six to twelve months later, of what is often an extremely long and detailed record of what you went through – it is not unusual for a statement to stretch to over 40 pages. Indeed, given the nature of trials of sexual offenders and the way they are carried out, it is imperative that, as the chief witness for the prosecution, you are as informed and prepared as it is possible for you to be.

Identification
If the man is arrested, you may be called on to attend an identification parade at the police station, in which you will have to point him out from a line of men.

Withdrawing charges
Perhaps no clearer example exists of our lack of control over the events of a prosecution than when we try to 'stop the ball rolling' once it has been started. You might wish to do so if, for instance, you were unsure about reporting in the first place. You may subsequently realise you do not wish to go through with a full prosecution, and that you would like to get out as quickly and with as little fuss as possible.

It is the experience of rape crisis centres that most women do not have much idea of what is actually involved in reporting and carrying through the prosecution of a sexual offence. Discovering later exactly what lies ahead, it is hardly surprising that many women feel they cannot face going through to the end and indeed regret ever having begun. However, once having set the process in motion, it is often not easy to stop it, and the further it has gone the more difficult it can be.

If you do decide to withdraw your complaint, you may get various reactions from your investigating police officers.

If, for instance, they have doubted from the beginning that the case is strong enough to get a conviction, they may be relieved at being asked to halt proceedings. They may even suggest along the way (sometimes subtly, sometimes not) that you might be better off withdrawing.

If, on the other hand, they are keen to go ahead with a prosecution (they may, for instance, recognise the man as someone who has committed multiple offences in the vicinity), they can make it extremely difficult for you not to co-operate. They might threaten a prosecution for wasting police time (rarely carried out, but the threat is suitably frightening); they may use emotional blackmail, by hinting that if the rapist goes free, and subsequently commits further crimes, you are in some way to blame; they might appeal to your 'civic duty', i.e. that you are in a position to help others, and the police cannot do their job without the assistance of members of the public such as you. The psychological disadvantage of any woman in such a situation is obvious and in theory you can be compelled by law to attend as a witness (see Chapter 5, Committal Proceedings). However, in practice it is more likely that the police would not be inclined to proceed with such a reluctant chief witness.

The most important aspect of withdrawing a complaint is the signing of a formal withdrawal form. Unless you have done this yourself, the case will proceed. It sometimes happens that a woman tells the officer in charge of her case that she wants to withdraw. He may well agree, or at least appear to. But if you have not actually signed the form, having first read it carefully to make sure it is what you think it is, then you have not withdrawn.

There have also been instances of women being effectively tricked into signing withdrawal forms by police uninterested in pursuing a case. Simply by being led to believe that a signature is needed on one more form, and then she can go home, a woman will sign without reading what it is she is signing. Too late – once this is done it is most unlikely that the police will ever destroy the form. The case is therefore officially dropped. The message is clear: *never* sign anything without reading it carefully.

Not reporting

The reasons why many women choose not to report to the police may already be clear. A medical examination which can feel like another assault, hours of intensive and often aggressive questioning understandably deter many of us, even without looking ahead to the probable court appearance later. Many woman have been threatened with further violence if they tell the police, or even if not explicitly, are justifiably afraid of the rapist and/or his friends and family. For some of us, the time limitations on reporting may rule it out as other considerations take priority – finding a safe place to stay if you're afraid of further violence, getting medical treatment if you're badly hurt (see Chapter 6 for casualty wards and reporting).

However, if you do not wish to report there are certain implications of making such a decision that it is important to be aware of. Reporting to the police is, of course, the only legal channel available by which you can try to obtain society's recognition of what has happened to you as a serious crime. It is this fact that makes the initial decision so difficult – together with the fact that it is usually irreversible. If, for instance, you decide not to report, you cannot change your mind weeks or months later. Often women cannot face reporting immediately after an assault but feel much better able to cope, say, a week or two later. It is only fair to point out the difficulties involved in trying to drum up interest from the police after such a lapse of time. While the police view on time lapse before reporting seems unclear – when pushed they generally make 'as soon as possible' noises – it is very rare for a case to be taken up if reported at this stage. The reason given for not proceeding would doubtless be 'lack of forensic evidence'. However the underlying reason appears often to be a total lack of belief. This is evident in the often harsh and sceptical treatment meted out by so many police officers, even to women who report within *hours* of an assault.[7]

So the first problem facing you if you choose not to report is the possibility of subsequently feeling that your only method of redress has slipped through your fingers, that he has got away with it. This may be accompanied by feelings of self-doubt and guilt – did I make the right decision? If this happens you need to hang on to the knowledge that the original decision was made for good reason; that it is an enormously difficult one at the best of times. To consciously make the decision at all is a courageous step – whatever you decide is right *for you* at the time.

Another problem is other people's reactions. Pressure may come from friends or family who do not agree with your decision, and may criticise or even not believe you if you choose not to bring in the police. It is of course your decision alone to make – it is you who will have to live with the consequences either way. If you choose not to report, for whatever reasons, your decision should be respected.

One final point: if you do not report to the police, you are unlikely to receive Criminal Injuries Compensation (see Chapter 5).

Complaints against police officers

There are various reasons why you might consider making a complaint against police officers investigating your case. They might include:

(a) slowness or lack of interest in taking up the complaint. For example, where the man's whereabouts are known both to you and the police, but they make no apparent attempt to question him;

(b) particularly insulting or insensitive treatment of you in the police station during questioning, for example, being moralistic and judgmental rather than simply doing their job;

(c) unnecessarily oppressive, callous or harsh treatment, for example, being questioned by unnecessary numbers of different officers, who perhaps display a vicarious interest in the details of the case;

(d) lack of vigilance in carrying out a proper investigation, for example, not making sure your clothes are removed for testing, or that you return to the police doctor when appropriate for recording of evidence of bruising;

(e) giving out confidential information about the case or your identity to the media;

(f) pressurising you to withdraw your complaint when you wish to proceed. (For more examples, see 'Rape: Police and Forensic Practice', RCCP, 1978.)

The procedure

In the light of recent events concerning police behaviour, police complaints procedure is currently being reviewed – and hopefully improved. However for the moment the procedure is broadly as set out below.

Metropolitan Police District of London   If at any time during contact with the police you have cause for complaint, it should be made firstly to the officer in charge of the station. Ask to see or speak to him in private, and do not be put off with speaking to anyone else. *Make sure* you have the correct name, rank and number of the officer(s) concerned. If, for example, you speak to someone on the telephone about whom you then wish to complain, you must know who it was you spoke to.

If the officer's explanation is unsatisfactory, you should then write in as much detail as possible to:

Complaints Investigation Department
New Scotland Yard
Broadway
London SW1.

You will be contacted by that Department and asked about your complaint. You should then receive a written explanation. If your complaint has been substantiated you should be told the results, for example, that the officer concerned has been reprimanded or demoted (depending on the seriousness of the charge).

If you are still not satisfied, you can then complain to your MP, or the Home Secretary.

Outside London   The procedure should be as follows:

(*a*) complain in the first instance to the officer in charge of the station;

(*b*) if unsatisfactory, the Chief Superintendent of your town;

(*c*) if still unsatisfactory, the Chief Constable for the metropolitan district, or county;

(d) finally, the Complaints Investigation Department, as above.

If you don't feel up to going through the first stages *(a)* and *(b)*, you can try just complaining to the Chief Constable and the Complaints Investigation Department. The official police procedure for complaints – the Complaints Investigation Department – is an internal body, therefore it is a case of police investigating police.

The relationship between most women and their investigating officers is a fragile one, and the degree of intimidation is such that it is unthinkable for the majority of us caught up in such a relationship to even contemplate making a formal complaint. Such a move is clearly a risk that women cannot afford to take as long as no alternative prosecution procedure exists.

5
Court

If you report rape to the police and they decide to take up the case, there will be two court hearings at which you may have to be present. If you report a 'lesser offence', for example, indecent assault, you may have to attend Magistrates' Court where the entire trial can be held. If the man is caught and charged with rape he will, as soon as possible after arrest, appear at Magistrates' Court for committal. This is a preliminary hearing at which the magistrates decide whether or not there is enough evidence to bring the case before a jury at Crown Court. You may or may not have to appear at the committal (see different types below), but you will certainly have to attend Crown Court unless the man pleads guilty. Even if he does plead guilty, he is entitled to change his plea at any time, so you may well be told to turn up anyway in case he changes his mind at the last minute. The Crown Court trial will usually take place six months to a year after committal.

Throughout the process your role will be 'chief witness for the prosecution' (see p. 35) and the man's will be the 'accused' or the 'defendant'. The main actors in court are the two barristers or 'counsel', one on the police's (and your) side ('prosecution counsel') and one on the man's side ('defence counsel'). The man will have met defence counsel before any court appearance to discuss how to fight the case, how to present himself in court, how to answer questions, and so on. You, however, will have no access to the prosecution counsel – your only contact will be with the police officer in charge of the case.

Court procedure

There are several general points which apply both to Crown Court and to those Magistrates' Court hearings at which you have to attend.

(a) Depending on the particular court facilities, you may find yourself, especially if the police do not accompany you to court, sharing a waiting room with the defendant's friends or family, and in exceptional cases, with the defendant himself. This will obviously be extremely distressing, particularly if there is the possibility of any threatening behaviour towards you. An attempt ought therefore to be made – by your officer in charge – to find out exactly what the arrangements will be.

(b) The defendant remains in court (in the dock, in Crown Court with at least one guard) for the entire trial, regardless of what is going on. You will therefore have a clear view of him, and he of you, both while you are giving evidence in the witness box, and wherever else in court you might be sitting.

(c) Unless circumstances are exceptional (for example, if the details of the case are particularly gruesome and/or the complainant is a young child) the court will be open to the public (who often sit in the gallery above and overlooking the court). Thus there may be – at least in Crown Court – some 20 or more people, and the jury, present in court. In the Magistrates' Court, the gallery will probably be at the back of the court and hold 10–20 people. If the judge directs that the public gallery be cleared (he is the only one who can), this is known as a hearing 'in camera'. It can be for the whole or part only of the proceedings.

(d) There will also be present members of the press. They sit in a special place of their own, and will normally remain there for the entire proceedings.

(e) As a witness, you are not permitted to speak except in answer to the questions at any time during proceedings. You cannot therefore reply to, comment on, or dispute anything you might hear said about you by anyone. You may only: (a) ask permission to speak of the magistrates or judge, while you are in the witness box, which they may or may not grant; or (b) speak to your officer in charge during any periods of recess, if you want to comment on or dispute anything that has happened up to that point, or if you have any general queries. He will make any necessary decisions on what to do.

(f) You should not speak about the trial to anyone unconnected with it, or any other witnesses, while it is in progress (you will probably be told this by your officer in charge anyway). If defence counsel has any inkling that a witness – especially the *chief* one – has been tampered with in any way by any outside influence, he may cause a huge fuss and demand that the case be thrown out, or re-tried.

Committal proceedings (Magistrates' Court)

The committal will usually take place 2–4 weeks after arrest of the suspect(s) (longer in London than elsewhere). The man does not have to enter a plea at this point and can ask for legal aid, someone to represent him and bail. If the magistrates commit the case for trial at Crown Court, he may be remanded on bail, which means he is released, with certain conditions, until the trial or remanded in custody, which means he will remain in prison until the trial. If the magistrates decide there is not enough evidence to put the case forward for trial by jury, that is it. The case will proceed no further, and the prosecution has no right of appeal. In other words there is nothing more you, the police or the prosecution counsel can do.

There are three possible types of committal – the defence counsel makes the choice.

Section 6(2)[1] *(also called a 'new style' or 'quick committal')*   There is no reason for you to have to attend a Section 6(2). Basically all those involved (prosecution and defence counsels, and magistrates) agree on the evidence submitted; there is no consideration or dispute of evidence at this stage.

Bail is granted or refused, the prosecution produces exhibits (which are numbered and labelled), and the case is committed – or not – to Crown Court for trial. The entire process is likely to be fairly brief.

Section 6(1) 'Paper committal'[2]   You may have to be present. This is similar to a Section 6(2). It involves statements – all or some – being read aloud in court. The defence counsel can then argue that there is insufficient evidence on which to try the accused, if he is pleading not guilty.

Section 6(1)[3] *(sometimes called 'old-style' or 'old-fashioned')* You must be present. This is a full 'dress-rehearsal' of the case and how it will proceed in Crown Court, so that although it is the most harrowing, you will at least have a good idea of what to expect. The defence has the right to withhold its defence witness(es) and not give any evidence at all. It is therefore able to see all the weak points in the other side, without giving away any of its own intended procedures.

Everything said in court is recorded, most often by a shorthand writer. Your statement will be read back to you, having been recorded, and you will be asked to verify that it is a true account of what you said, and to sign it. If anything is inaccurate you should try not to be afraid to say so. A copy of the statement will then be given to the defence lawyers, to be used in Crown Court where you will be re-examined, and your evidence there may be checked against that given at committal.

Trial by jury (Crown Court)

If agreed by the magistrates, the trial will be committed to Crown Court. The particular court and date will be decided later. In London, the average time lapse between committal and Crown Court is approximately 12 months. Elsewhere it is likely to be less – perhaps six months. It will always be shorter if the accused is kept in custody; custody cases are usually given priority to avoid the cost of keeping an accused in prison for prolonged periods awaiting trial.

The majority of cases coming to Crown Court will not have a fixed date on which to begin. So, short of these broad guidelines, you are unlikely to have any idea of the starting date. However, if the time lapse continues beyond 12 months you have good cause for complaint, and should do so, preferably with some support. Not all cases are given a fixed date, but you should be told in which week the trial will start. When a case is on the 'warned list', it may come to court any day that week, or none of them. If court time is available, it will then be slotted in at the last minute, which can leave you with as little as 15–24 hours notice. You should be informed, in person, by at least two police officers. You will be summonsed to appear as a witness, which means you are compelled by law to attend. You should inform your officer in charge if you expect to be unavailable for any reason, for example, holidays. You may only avoid attendance if:

(a) you are unwell and produce a medical certificate exempting you;

(b) extremely sympathetic police allow you to drop charges (see Chapter 4, Withdrawing Charges);

(c) the defendant pleads guilty (see beginning of this chapter).

Court layout   Briefly, Crown Court will be laid out as follows:

(a) The judge, usually wearing red robes and wig, sits in an elevated position, beneath which are usually one or two clerks of the court, wearing black robes. He will take his own notes throughout proceedings, which he will then use in his summing-up, towards the end.

(b) Usually opposite the judge, on the other side of the room, is the dock, where sit the defendant and guards.

(c) Along one side of the court, in two rows, sits the jury. They have the clearest view of the whole court, since in effect the entire 'performance' is for their benefit. The witness box will usually be alongside them, but sometimes across the room.

(d) The witness box will contain – usually – a seat, a microphone, and a glass of water (provided and replenished by a clerk or usher, also in black robes). It is usually fairly near, but below, the judge.

(e) Between the judge and the dock, on floor level, will be several rows of chairs behind desks. Here sit counsel (barristers, in black gowns and wigs), instructing solicitors and their clerks, and police officers directly connected with the case, who are not witnesses in it.

The jury   The jury normally consists of 12 people[4] chosen from the general public. They can, in theory, be anyone, of either sex, whose name is on the electoral register (over the voting age, but under 65). No-one can choose who must go on any particular jury; however, either prosecution or defence counsel can challenge jury members if they wish, before proceedings begin. This means they can object to particular jurors, or the entire jury.

(a) The *defence* counsel may challenge three jurors *per defendant* without giving reasons. So that if there are three men on trial

together, 9 of the 12 jury members can be challenged, and replaced. It is not unusual for women jurors to be challenged. The *prosecution* may ask any juror to 'stand by' without showing cause, until the jury panel is used up.

(b) If the entire jury is challenged, the grounds for so doing must be specified in writing – this hardly ever happens.

The trial

Once initial proceedings – swearing-in of the jury, and so on – are over, you will usually be called as first prosecution witness. You will not have been in the court before then. Prosecution counsel ('your' side) will take you through your statement (you should ask to see a copy before proceedings begin, if you do not already have one – it is best not to consult it in court[5]). Defence counsel will then cross-examine you. Basically he will have a different version of events (given him by the man). His job is to question you very closely on every point in your statement he senses to be weak, or at least arguable. He will try to make you out to be an unreliable witness, if not a liar, so that the case against his client can be shown to be weak (hopefully, in his eyes, weak enough to be thrown out). The means he will use to do this are less than laudable; questioning may well be along the following lines:

How did he touch you?
Did you have a period at the time?
Did you have a climax? (This is to try to defuse the violence, as well as prove consent.)
Was he circumcised?
Did you ask him to use his fingers?
Why didn't you try to escape?
You enjoyed it, didn't you?
You asked him to bugger you, didn't you?
You slept with his friend the first night you met him, didn't you?
You go into pubs alone, don't you?
. . . etc., etc., etc.

The intention is generally to undermine your confidence, confuse you about the sequence of events (so that you might contradict yourself), and cast a slur on your character.

If the defence counsel casts a slur on your character he runs the risk that the prosecution counsel may be able to cross-examine the defendant on his character. In practice, defendants are often allowed to cast a slur on your character, without their character being brought into question. Counsel are normally extremely experienced in their questioning methods, although not necessarily particularly good, or clever. It is unwise to try and outwit them. All you can do is answer questions as straightforwardly and as truthfully as possible. You may – if you are feeling brave enough – ask the judge something like 'Do I really have to answer that question? Why is it relevant?' You must, however, abide by the judge's answer.

After your cross-examination is over, you are permitted to leave the court unless there is a chance that defence counsel may want to recall you for further questioning. If so, you will be told not to leave the area, or make yourself unavailable, or possibly even to remain in court. You are also entitled to remain in court for the entire trial. However this is sometimes frowned upon by police officers, who fear the jury may think that the attack cannot have been so bad if you are happy to stay and listen to the whole proceedings.

The chief prosecution witness will normally be followed by other prosecution witnesses (the police, police doctor and so on), all of whom will be questioned and cross-questioned in the same way. It is then the turn of the defence, whose witnesses should be similarly cross-examined by the prosecution (including, of course, the defendant(s)). Defence witnesses can be witnesses to the crime, or character witnesses. The prosecution then sums up its case, followed by the defence who does likewise.

In each step of court proceedings the defence will always follow the prosecution. This is to give the defendant as much opportunity as possible to refute all the charges being made against him. In theory, the defence does not really have to say anything at all since the accused's innocence is assumed from the start. The job of proving he is *not* innocent always rests with the prosecution. In practice this means that the woman is assumed to be making false allegations unless the prosecution can prove otherwise.

After both counsels have summed up, the judge then 'sums up' the entire case. It is his job to tell the jury the law, review all the evidence, and point out to the jury things they should bear in mind when making their decision. He can give his opinion on the facts, but should tell the jury they are not bound by it. The jury *is* bound by what the judge tells them about the law. The jury retires for as long as necessary, then comes back into court and announces the verdict.

The verdict

If the jury gives a 'guilty' verdict, the judge will then pass sentence. The defence has a right to appeal against conviction and/or sentence if the man pleaded not guilty, and against sentence if he pleaded guilty.

If the jury return a verdict of 'not guilty' however, the prosecution has no right of appeal. This means that neither you nor the police can do anything to argue, or to have the case re-examined. A verdict of 'not guilty', after enduring the anguish of a court case in which you may have felt that it was you that was on trial, is extremely distressing. It may feel like a slap in the face, a denial of all that you have suffered.

If this happens, it may help a little to know that a 'not guilty' verdict does not necessarily mean that the jury think the man is innocent. When a judge sums up at the end of the trial, amongst other things he will instruct the jury that unless they are sure 'beyond all reasonable doubt' (or words to that effect) that he is guilty, they must return a verdict of 'not guilty'. So even if the jury is, say, fairly sure of guilt, that is not enough. A verdict of 'not guilty' means not that the jury necessarily doubt his guilt but that there is not enough evidence to convict.

If the jury cannot agree after at least two hours and ten minutes, the judge can accept a majority of ten to two, or can order a re-trial.

Sentencing

Only after the jury has given a 'guilty' verdict, can any previous convictions the man has had be read in court, to be taken into account in the judge's sentence. (Up till then a past record may not be mentioned or implied for fear of influencing the jury's decision – ironic given that the woman's perfectly legal sexual past is so often considered fair game.) The sentence the judge decides on will also be influenced therefore by factors other than the seriousness of the crime – other offences the man has committed, his age, and anything else the judge in his personal opinion considers relevant (such as any previous relationship you had with the man, or whether the judge attributes any responsibility to you).

In January 1982 Judge Bertrand Richards at Ipswich Crown Court provoked a public outcry by giving only a fine to a man found guilty of rape, justifying this by claiming that the woman concerned was 'guilty of contributory negligence' by hitchhiking at night. 'Contributory negligence' is a legal concept which applies only to the civil law, and *not* to the criminal law at all. Although most judges are sharper than to make their personal prejudices so explicit, it is not at all uncommon for them to deny the seriousness of rape.

In 1980, 19 percent of the men found guilty of rape in England and Wales were not sentenced to immediate imprisonment but received sentences such as probation orders, borstal training, suspended sentences or fines. Of those receiving prison sentences, 50.5 percent got three years or less, and only 6.2 percent[6] got over seven years.

Compensation

The Criminal Injuries Compensation Board exists to provide monetary compensation to victims of violent crimes where personal injury has been sustained. Information and application forms can be obtained from:

Criminal Injuries Compensation Board
10–12 Russell Square
London WC1B 5EN
Tel: 01-636 2812/4201

The Board covers the whole of Great Britain. Its members (17, two of whom are women) are legally qualified and are appointed by the Home Secretary.

Who can claim Any woman or girl (if under 18, parent or guardian on her behalf) who has been sexually assaulted in any way can make a claim. Though in theory you need not have reported the crime to the police to make a claim, Board members will take into account whether you have or not when considering your claim. They are more likely to make an award if you have reported, though the case need not have proceeded to court, nor need there have been a conviction. The Board states:

> The Board may withhold or reduce compensation if they consider that –
> *(a)* the applicant has not taken, without delay, all reasonable steps to inform the police, or any other authority considered by the Board to be appropriate for the purpose, of the circumstances of the injury and to co-operate with the police or other authority in bringing the offender to justice. . .[7]

The scheme *does not* cover British subjects injured abroad.

What is covered Compensation is paid for pain and suffering, injury, shock, loss of earnings including those resulting from consequent pregnancy, and if appropriate, the expense of childbirth resulting from rape. Awards do *not* cover maintenance towards such a child.

When to claim You must make your claim within three years of the incident. Only in 'exceptional' cases is this requirement waived.

Award figures The minimum award paid is £400, except where the violence occurred within the family, where it is £500 (not taxable). In the experience of the London Rape Crisis Centre recent awards have been in the region of £3000. NB If you are awarded more than £2000 and are claiming social security, your benefits will be withdrawn.

The procedure You must apply in writing. You do not have to attend in person unless you appeal against a decision (see below). Although the form is not especially difficult it may seem somewhat daunting; it may be worth enlisting the help of, say, a rape crisis centre to fill it in. A solicitor might also be helpful, but a legal qualification is not necessary.

The application is assessed by *one* Board member who will decide whether or not an award should be made. If it is successful, and you feel the award is satisfactory (i.e. not so low as to be an insult) you have three months in which to accept it. If you are not satisfied you can appeal by applying for a hearing. (The Board may decide to hold a hearing themselves.)

Appeal   You might decide to appeal if you receive an award you think is too low, or if you receive no award at all. You will then have to attend a private hearing, relatively informal, before three Board members (often one is a woman). If any reports of such hearings are published they are anonymous. You do not need to have a legal representative; you may simply appear on your own behalf. It is possible to get legal aid for advice beforehand, but not to cover the cost of legal representation.

An application put by a solicitor or barrister will on the whole do better than one which is not; the Board are, after all, members of the same profession. A member of the Board's staff is present to call witnesses and to cross-examine you and your witnesses.

All witnesses, both to the crime and to the state of the woman afterwards, are usually invited. This means that as well as police, doctors, and other witnesses, it is possible that the assailant may be asked to attend, if his identity is known (although the Board does not insist that he does). The Board will cross-examine you, and your evidence will also be open to question by anyone else concerned. Often a medical *report* will be sufficient and the doctor(s) need not attend.

The decision by the Board will be made on the spot, *and is final.*[8] If you appeal against too low an award, the one big risk is that the Board could make a renewed award that is actually *lower* than the original one.

Time   The Board can take up to six months to make a decision on a claim. In a situation where the case is proceeding to court, and the Board is aware that a court case is pending, it will not make its decision until after the trial. However this does not mean that it is waiting to hear a 'guilty' verdict before making an award; in fact the Board says that its testing of evidence is not as rigorous as that of a criminal court. Though it will wait until the trial decision – for reasons unfathomable – it does have discretion to make an interim award. (During the period April 1978 to March 1979, 1107 final decisions and 105 interim awards were made.)

On the face of it, this all seems fine, and relatively easy. However the 'small print' of the CICB's information sheets reveals the underlying judgmental attitudes common throughout the legal profession:

> The Board may withhold or reduce compensation if they consider that. . .
>
> *(c)* having regard to the conduct of the applicant before, during or after the events giving rise to the claim, or to his character and way of life . . . it is inappropriate that a full award, or any award at all, be granted . . .
>
> In order to determine whether there was any responsibility, either because of provocation or otherwise, on the part of the victim, the Board will scrutinise with particular care all applications in respect of sexual offences or other offences which arise out of a sexual relationship . . . In such cases the Board will especially have regard to any delay that has occurred in submitting the application.[9]

In other words, the Board takes it upon itself to judge a woman's culpability in the assault, and may deny you, in part or in whole, the chance of financial compensation as a result. There is something particularly distasteful in this form of censure since, in effect, women can be 'rewarded' or not for 'good behaviour' (or more correctly, absence of '*bad* behaviour').

Many of us also feel a further distaste for the whole idea of financial compensation as a result of rape. Whatever price is put on emotional distress, money can never compensate for being raped.

The amounts the Board awards reflect the general lack of seriousness with which women's experiences of sexual violence are treated throughout society. In 1981, a woman of 17, raped three times when she was pregnant and consequently unable to continue with the pregnancy, was awarded £5000. In the same year a man of 42 who was kicked in the testicles, receiving no lasting injury but suffering from psychological impotence, was awarded £22,500, later reduced to £17,500.[10]

6
Medical Information

Whatever else you do after being raped, it is essential to be aware of the possible physical effects on your body and to deal with them as soon as possible. Aside from bruising, cuts or other injuries, if you were raped vaginally, pregnancy is a possibility. Sexually transmitted (or venereal) diseases are a possible result of vaginal, anal and/or oral rape.

It is hard to think about these things immediately, but knowing what is going on in your body enables you to begin to take back control over it. VD is easily cured if detected early. And if you are at risk of pregnancy, the earlier you seek advice the wider are your choices of what to do about it.

Shock

Some degree of shock usually follows any injury or traumatic experience. Physical reactions can range over a wide spectrum, including uncontrollable shivering or shaking, inability to think, your mind going blank, a dry mouth, loss of muscle control which can lead to defecation or urination, inability to sit down or try to relax, hysterical laughter, crying, twitching of facial muscles and numbness.

If you have been raped you may have any or all of these reactions, and you may have them immediately or some time later (delayed shock). They may occur just for an hour or two, or may last on and off, or for longer. Apart from getting treatment for injuries, there is little you can do but keep warm (avoiding direct heat or sudden changes in temperature which can cause fainting), drink a cup of tea, and allow yourself to cry if you want to. It is a good idea to have a woman friend with you if possible. This type of shock will take its course and pass in time.

It is possible too that feelings of numbness, or distance from what has happened and is happening around you, may occur if you were drugged. They may also follow from 'switching off' as a means of surviving or enduring the rape.

The term 'shock' can also be used for a different and much more serious condition which can be caused by very severe injuries. Shock in this sense is a state of collapse, in which a woman is unable to function though she may possibly be semi-conscious. It is a medical emergency requiring hospital attention.

Injuries

If any part of your body is badly injured, it is important to go to a hospital casualty department for immediate treatment. If, for instance, you have severe vaginal bleeding (heavier than a period and continuous), you should not wait to see a GP but get straight to hospital. You will, in this case, have to tell the hospital what has happened or they may not be able to treat you effectively.

Any cuts or tears are best treated quickly – if you are suffering from pain and/or bleeding you should try and see a doctor as soon as possible. If you have a GP you like, it is worth visiting her or him if you have only slight injuries – however GPs will usually refer you to the local casualty department if stitches are required.

If you are worried about the possibility of minor injuries – vaginal or anal tears, for example – the VD clinic should be able to tell you. Since you have an internal examination there anyway this may save you going through it twice. However, the VD clinic will not do stitching so you may have to go to hospital as well.

Pregnancy

Assessing the risk

It is a dangerous myth that you cannot get pregnant from being raped.

Getting pregnant has nothing to do with being relaxed or enjoying intercourse. It also has nothing to do with whether or not you have had intercourse before. If there was a possibility of any penis to vagina or vulva contact, there is a risk of pregnancy, although slighter if the man did not ejaculate.

How high the risk is depends largely on what stage in your menstrual cycle you are at when you are raped. Knowing how serious the risk is will help you to decide whether to try and obtain 'morning after' contraception or to have a pregnancy test at a later date (see below). It is unwise though to rely on being in a 'safe' part of your cycle – if there is any risk you should seek advice.

Pregnancy occurs when the egg (ovum) released, usually once a month, from a woman's ovary is fertilised by the man's sperm. The ovum can be fertilised up to about two days after it is released (i.e. after ovulation). Sperm can stay alive in a woman's body usually up to 72 hours (occasionally for up to five days) and can fertilise an ovum at any point during this time.

The risk of pregnancy is greater if you are raped about two weeks before your next period is due, i.e. around the time you ovulate. If you have a regular menstrual cycle, it is easier to calculate the risk – in a 28 day cycle you are at highest risk for about a week in the middle. With shorter or longer cycles, or if your periods are irregular, it is more difficult to know, and even if your cycle is regular you are unlikely to be certain of the time you ovulate.

If you have not yet started your periods there may still be a risk, since you do not bleed until after you first ovulate. Similarly, if you have reached the menopause and your periods appear to have stopped, this is often not a reliable sign of infertility – many women think their periods have finished, then have another after a gap of, say, six months.

Obviously if you are on the pill or have a coil the risk of pregnancy is much less. Contraceptive pills, if taken regularly, are over 99 percent effective and the coil over 97 percent effective in preventing pregnancy. However, the pill can be rendered ineffective if you have suffered recently from vomiting or diarrhoea, or by taking certain antibiotics – in any of these circumstances, you should seek extra advice.

Post-coital ('morning after') pregnancy prevention

It is possible now in Britain to get 'morning after' contraception – misleadingly named as it is still effective if used considerably later than 24 hours after the rape – to prevent pregnancy. There are two methods available, the post-coital ('morning after') pill and post-coital IUD (intra-uterine device or coil). They work during the interval between ovulation and implantation, by preventing the fertilised ovum from implanting itself in the womb. They are therefore methods of interception rather than abortion. The interval between ovulation and implantation is approximately five days – three days for the fertilised egg to move down the fallopian tube into the uterus and about two days inside the uterus before implantation occurs.

Post-coital contraception is worth considering if you were raped at the time in your menstrual cycle when the risk of pregnancy is highest, and if there was no chance of you being pregnant already. It is not yet widely available – it is worth appraoching GPs and family planning clinics although their responses vary. Alternatively, most of the private, charitable agencies offer post-coital services. Neither method should be used without medical supervision. With both methods you should be asked to return to the doctor after about four weeks to check that there is no continuing pregnancy.

Post-coital methods are a fairly recent development. Although current methods are a great improvement on early ones, there are both limitations and side effects.

Post-coital ('morning after') pill   This method can be used up to 72 hours after the rape, but it is best to get the prescription as soon as possible, as some evidence suggests that the effectiveness decreases towards the end of this period.

The prescription most commonly used at the time of writing is a combined oestrogen/progestogen pill available as an oral contra-ceptive in the UK under the brand names Eugynon 50 or Ovran. The dose is two pills (ethinyloestradiol 100 micrograms, levon-orgestrel 500 micrograms), followed by another two pills twelve hours later.

Earlier methods used a very high dose of oestrogen (ethinyloestradiol or stilboestral) taken for five days. This is sometimes still prescribed. It has dangerous and unpleasant side-effects and should be avoided. The current method using the combined pill described above contains only ¹⁄₁₂₅ of the dose of oestrogen prescribed in the earlier methods.

Taking the combined pill can radically alter your menstrual cycle. Bleeding can be expected from immediately after you take the first two pills, until up to a month later. However, it is imperative that you take both sets of pills, irrespective of when the bleeding starts. Also, if you do not start to bleed straight away, or if bleeding coincides with the normal time of your period, this does not mean that the pills have been ineffective.

Other side effects of the combined pill (Eugynon 50 or Ovran) are nausea (which about 25 percent of women suffer from), and vomiting (about 15 percent),[1] and possibly headaches, drowsiness and breast tenderness, but these are rare. You may be prescribed an anti-emetic as well to combat nausea. If you have a history of high blood pressure, vaginal or uterine cancer or sickle-cell anaemia, you may be advised not to take the pill.

The method is approximately 97–98 percent effective, and failure is very unlikely if the pills are taken within 48 hours. However if it does fail there is a slight chance that the foetus will be damaged and you may therefore be advised to have an abortion. Some doctors may require you to sign a consent form saying you will have an abortion if the method fails before they prescribe the post-coital pill.

Post-coital IUD The IUD may be recommended if you are outside the 72-hour period for the post-coital pill or if it is unsafe for you to take the pill. The IUD is best inserted as soon as possible, but is effective in preventing pregnancy up to five days after the rape. It is an ordinary IUD (coil) as used in contraception, and should be inserted by some-one trained to do so, usually a doctor. When you return for a check-up, it can be removed. The post-coital IUD has a very low failure rate.

The major disadvantage of the IUD is that the internal probing necessary for insertion can be traumatic so soon after being raped. Insertion can also be painful, and you may feel nauseous for a few minutes or hours afterwards. Bleeding can last from a few hours to several days. Your next period should come at the expected time but it may be heavier and a little longer than usual.

Another problem is that if you have contracted a sexually transmitted disease, insertion of the IUD will push the infection further inside you – there is therefore a risk of contracting an infection of the fallopian tubes (salpingitis). Since the earliest you can have VD tests is three days after the rape, you will probably not know whether or not you have an infection at the time you have to decide about having an IUD .

If you feel at all unhappy about having an IUD inserted, you should not be pushed into doing so.

Pregnancy tests

Until recently, the earliest you could get a reliable pregnancy test was one month after conception or 14 days after a missed period. However, there are now special early tests which can be done from ten days after possible conception. They are not yet widely available, and there are different types effective at different times, some based on a urine sample only, some requiring a blood test too. Rape crisis centres should be able to give information on local availability.

The more commonly used test relies on picking up traces of a hormone which is produced during the first four months of pregnancy, but is not present in sufficient quantities for detection during the first month. This test is free from your GP or family planning clinic but you may have to wait a week for the result. Chemists who do this test generally give you the result in about 24 hours, as do the private agencies (see p. 138), but you have to pay. Wherever you go, you need to take an early-morning urine sample – from the first time you urinate that day – in a clean bottle labelled with your name.

There are also do-it-yourself pregnancy testing kits sold by chemists (who have been known to use them for their own testing service) – they are expensive and not always reliable. If you are pregnant and want to have an abortion, you will have to get another test done anyway. And if you think you may want an abortion on the National Health Service, it is best to see your GP or family planning clinic as soon as possible, even if you get a test done privately for speed. In Britain, Brook Advisory Centres (see Appendix 5) also do free pregnancy tests, give abortion advice and arrange NHS referral if required.

Although the most common symptom of pregnancy is a missed period, very occasionally you may have a light period but still be pregnant. Other common symptoms are nausea and vomiting, tender breasts, frequent urination and tiredness.

If you are pregnant

It is very distressing to find that you are pregnant from rape. On top of the trauma of the rape itself you will have to make decisions with long-term implications about a situation that you did not choose. What is happening to your body continues to be out of your control. It is important that you do decide what to do as soon as possible – whether to have an abortion or go ahead with the pregnancy, and if the latter whether or not to have the baby adopted. It is a hard decision but if left too long it may be too late to have an abortion and you may find yourself going ahead with the pregnancy without ever making a decision to do so. It helps to find someone to talk through your feelings and fears about the different options with before you decide (say a friend, Brook counsellor or RCC).

No one should be pressurised into having an abortion if they feel unhappy about it. It is rarely an easy choice. However, the implications of the choice after rape are very different from those when you have chosen to have intercourse. If you were raped, it is not in any degree your responsibility that you are pregnant. And going through a full pregnancy even if you then have the baby adopted is a heavy additional burden to carry, on top of the rape itself.

Having an abortion after rape can feel a relief – you are very clearly getting rid of one consequence of the rape, and may not be able to deal with other feelings arising from it until this is over. Alternatively you may have focused so much on being pregnant that when this is no longer a problem it may be a shock that there are other consequences, that you may still be feeling bad. If you would not in other circumstances have chosen an abortion, you may still have mixed feelings afterwards. Again, it is helpful to talk about them.

Some of us do not have a choice and for religious or other reasons are unable to consider an abortion. In this case you may think of having the baby adopted. Others want to keep the child. If you do, the child may well prove a constant reminder of the rape – which might be hard on both of you.

A further problem in deciding what to do is that if you have intercourse voluntarily shortly before or after the rape and become pregnant, you may not know who the father is. Date of conception can be pinpointed fairly accurately by a scan to within about a week. If that is not accurate enough, you may have to live with that uncertainty if you decide to go ahead with the pregnancy.

Getting an abortion

The earlier you have an abortion the easier and safer it is. Legally in Britain you can have an abortion until you are up to 28 weeks pregnant. In practice, it is difficult to get one on the National Health Service after 16 weeks and almost impossible to get one anywhere after 22 weeks.

In addition, the number of weeks is counted not from the date of conception but from the first day of your last menstrual period, which may add two or three weeks to the actual length of time. Arranging an abortion through the NHS takes time – it is important to start the process as soon as possible as it may end up being too late to get one. In many hospitals 'too late' is as early as 12 weeks pregnant. Going to a private agency is simpler, quicker and often more pleasant, but an early abortion costs about £100 and later ones even more.

National Health Service

Most hospitals take abortion referrals only from GPs or the family planning linic doctors. If you've seen your GP shortly after the attack, she or he is more likely to be helpful if you request an abortion. You have to have a 'green form' signed by two consenting doctors before you can get an abortion for any reason. Usually your GP will be one and will send it with a letter of referral to the local hospital. You will then see a gynaecologist at the hospital who makes the final decision. Alternatively, the GP may just write a letter of referral and you will then have to see two doctors at the hospital.

If your GP is anti-abortion and/or doesn't believe you've been raped and refuses to refer you, you can try other GPs until you find one who will, but that can be a time-consuming business. Family planning clinics and Brook Advisory Centres can also refer for NHS abortions, as can the private agencies, although they deal mainly with their own (fee-paying) clinics.

Facilities for abortion vary greatly from hospital to hospital, as do the attitudes of doctors and gynaecologists. Even within the same gynaecology unit, the doctors may have very different attitudes. It is worth checking with the GP referring you about which gynaecologists are likely to be most helpful, and arranging your appointment accordingly. If you see one who refuses your request, it may be difficult to see another in the same hospital. However you can go to another hospital in the same catchment area if there is another one with a gynaecology unit.

Some hospitals have a medical social worker who sees women seeking abortions before they see the gynaecologist. They are usually sympathetic and supportive.

If you have an NHS abortion and have to stay in hospital, there is a possibility that you will be put in a maternity or gynaecology ward with women who have had miscarriages for instance, and may encounter some hostility from staff and patients. The attitude to women who have been raped is often sceptical.

Some areas now have day-care units where, if you have an early abortion, you can have it done and return home the same day.

Private agencies

If you cannot get an abortion on the NHS you may have to go to one of the private agencies (see Appendix 5). They are non-profitmaking organisations, but you do have to pay – from about £115 for an early abortion to nearly £300 for those performed later, at the time of writing.

The agencies provide counselling, so you get a chance to talk through your feelings about having an abortion first – if you decide against it you just pay the consultation fee. If you go ahead, you are given an appointment to attend a private clinic where all the other patients are also women having abortions, and the whole process is over in about ten days.

All the agencies have some system of helping with fees, occasionally with grants and more commonly loans, if you are in severe financial difficulty. You have to go through a fairly stiff means test though, and of course be prepared to repay loans.

Abortion methods

By and large the method of abortion used depends on how many weeks pregnant you are. However, practice varies from hospital to hospital and changes with new developments, so we can only give a rough guide here. For detailed information, see books listed at the end of this chapter.

The most common method of abortion, used between 6 and 12 weeks of pregnancy, is vacuum aspiration. This is the method used in day-care clinics. It takes about ten minutes and can be done under local or general anaesthetic. In hospitals you will usually stay overnight or sometimes two nights.

If it is too late for a vacuum aspiration, some hospitals will do abortion by D & C (dilation and curettage) up to 16 weeks. This is usually done under general anaesthetic. Not all hospitals do this operation but the private agencies offer it, and if you are over 12 weeks pregnant it is certainly preferable to waiting till 16 weeks for induction.

After 16 weeks, 'late abortions' are done by induction. This means that you are put on a drip (usually prostaglandin) to induce labour. You will get contractions (like when giving birth only more intense) and go into labour, possibly for several hours, before aborting. The whole process can take up to 12 hours. You may be alone when you abort, and you may see the foetus – this can be a very distressing experience.

The possible side effects of induction are nausea and diarrhoea.

You will also have to have a D & C under general anaesthetic after the abortion.

Occasionally, if induction has been or seems likely to be unsuccessful or dangerous, a hysterotomy is performed. This is an operation done on the same principles as a caesarian section birth – it is rare and can cause problems with future pregnancies.

Menstrual extraction (or very early abortion) is performed only in very few hospitals and clinics in Britain yet. It has to be done within about 14 days of missing a period. In the USA it is commonly done without a pregnancy test and is sometimes called menstrual regulation or pre-emptive abortion. In this way you never know whether you were pregnant or not. In the UK the abortion laws make it legal only after a positive pregnancy test. Although the increasing availability of special early tests makes menstrual extraction more possible, timing even then is extremely tight and it is difficult to get through the administrative hurdles in time.

Abortion for under-16s

Usually a girl under 16 needs her parents' permission to have an abortion, and technically even to have an internal examination. Legally this is a grey area – the General Medical Council says 'Where a minor requests treatment concerning a pregnancy or contraceptive advice the doctor should particularly have in mind the need to avoid impairing parental responsibility or family stability. The doctor should assess the patient's degree of parental dependence and seek to persuade the patient to involve the parents (or guardian or other person in loco parentis) from the earliest stage of consultation. If the patient refuses to allow a parent to be told, the doctor must observe the rule of professional secrecy in his management of the case.'[2] These guidelines do not mean that a doctor must go ahead and make it possible for a girl under 16 to have an abortion – he can refuse to treat her. However it does mean that a doctor *cannot* inform a girl's parents that she is pregnant without her permission.

Getting an internal examination without parental consent is not often a problem in practice – doctors can perform one 'in good faith';

in other words, if they believe it is clinically necessary and the girl doesn't want her parents informed.

Women visitors from abroad

It is difficult for women who are raped while visiting the UK to get an abortion on the NHS. You usually have to have registered with a local doctor before you know you are pregnant to get one. If you can afford it, it is easier to go for a private abortion.

Please see Appendix 5 for more information on this section.

Venereal disease (VD) or sexually transmitted diseases

It is very important for every woman who has been raped to go for a VD check-up soon afterwards – no one is immune from infection and if you catch a sexually transmitted disease this is entirely because the rapist had one. Getting VD from being raped has nothing to do with whether you have had sex before or not, or how many times, or with how many people. It is nothing to be ashamed of or embarrassed about.

You should have tests between three and seven days after the rape, but if you miss that time you can still have them later. Any infection will be easily treated if detected quickly, but if VD is left untreated it can cause serious internal damage. You cannot just wait and see if symptoms appear and assume that if there are not any, there is no infection – some sexually transmitted diseases show no symptoms until a fairly late stage. It is, of course, very upsetting to find you have VD. Being raped often leaves us feeling dirty anyway, and finding you have an infection of crabs, say, as well, is awful. Starting an effective course of treatment as soon as possible is the only way to get over this.

VD is often associated with promiscuity and many of us are made to feel embarrassed or ashamed of having such an infection, or even admitting the possibility, even when we have not chosen to have sexual intercourse. There are frightening myths – of incurable disease and insanity, the humiliation of bearing the marks of a life of immorality – allowed to persist by the embarrassed silence and ignorance surrounding VD. In fact many common venereal diseases are bacterial infections and are easily treated with a course of antibiotics, much as tonsillitis would be treated. They can be caught by sexual contact – genital, anal or oral – with a man who has the infection.

Where to go

VD clinics also have a rather distorted, somewhat shady image, which makes many women afraid to go for check-ups. The embarrassment we are made to feel for having such a disease is perpetuated by clinics being publicised in 'discreet' places such as public toilets. In fact most hospitals have a VD clinic (mostly called special clinics, or department of genito–urinary medicine) along with other out-patient clinics, and it is simply a place with the right equipment for effective diagnosis and specialist staff experienced in treating sexually transmitted diseases.

You can find out where your local clinic is from the phone book (under Venereal Diseases) or by ringing a hospital, health centre, Citizens' Advice Bureau or your GP. You can go to any clinic – it does not have to be one in your area. Some clinics have an appointment system and you have to phone in advance, at some you can just turn up and wait. It is best to phone and check clinic times even if you do not need an appointment – and if you would prefer to see a woman doctor, ask when there will be one on duty.

VD clinics are completely confidential – they will not tell your GP about your attendance unless you want them to. This applies even to girls under 16.

It is a good idea to have a friend go with you for support – as well as the questioning, it may be upsetting to be examined internally so soon after the rape. If you are worried about going and cannot find anyone to go with you, many clinics have a social worker or contact tracer who may be able to meet you when you arrive. (A contact tracer's job is to trace the 'partners' of patients who are found to have an infection.)

What happens at the clinic

At the clinic you will see a doctor who will ask about your general medical history and some questions about why you have come. While there are certain things the doctor will need to know – whether you were raped vaginally, orally or anally – in order to do the right tests, you should not have to give further details of what happened to you unless you wish to. You may well be asked however if you knew the rapist, and for his name if you did – this is so that if the tests are positive the clinic can contact him to ask him to come for treatment. There may be many reasons why you do not wish to give the name if you know it – safety, for example – and you do not have to. Your local RCC may be able to help, by asking the clinic in advance not to ask you more questions than is absolutely necessary.

The tests will include an internal examination, urine and blood tests. You should be prepared to produce a urine specimen at the clinic. Swabs are taken for samples from the vagina, cervix (neck of the womb), urethra (opening that leads from the bladder), anus and mouth, on which slide and culture tests are done. The slide tests are examined immediately at the clinic and the results given to you then. Culture tests, which are more accurate, take longer (three to seven days) and you will usually have to return to the clinic or ring them a week later for the results. You may also have to go back after 12 weeks for the blood test which is used to detect syphilis. It is important to go back even if you have not got symptoms.

If the results are positive, the doctor should explain exactly what the infection is and how it will be treated. Treatment usually consists of antibiotics – by injection, course of injections or course of tablets – and is continued until a negative test result (or sometimes two) is obtained. If you are allergic to any antibiotics, tell the doctor. It is important to complete the course of treatment prescribed even if any symptoms you had have disappeared.

If you went to a casualty department immediately after the rape you may well have been given a shot of penicillin or other antibiotic then. This is most likely to be done for wounds, and does not necessarily give protection against VD. You should still go to the special clinic, and tell the doctor what treatment, if any, you have had recently.

Common diseases

For full details of all the various infections, sexually transmitted and otherwise we suggest further reading (see the end of this chapter). Below, we mention briefly some of the most common infections women get after being raped. Symptoms are often similar for different infections and include: pain on passing urine, vaginal discharge, lower abdominal pelvic pain, itching, soreness, painful lumps or warts in the genital area.

We must stress again though that it is common to have an infection and show no symptoms at all for some time. You should *not* wait for symptoms to appear before having tests.

1. Gonorrhea (commonly called 'the clap') is a bacterial infection transmitted by vaginal, anal or oral intercourse, and is treated with antibiotics. If left untreated, complications can be serious.

2.NSU. (non-specific urethritis) is also called NSGI (non-specific genital infection). This is very common.

3. Trichomoniasis (trich) is transmitted by vaginal intercourse as well as in other non-sexual ways and treated with 'flagyl'. Flagyl can cause thrush (see below) and has other side effects. It should not be taken in large doses if you are pregnant.

4. Syphilis is a troponemal infection, which is a special form of bacterial infection which is very serious in its late stages. These however take many years of ignoring symptoms to reach. It is detected by a blood test which is not reliable until 12 weeks after exposure, and treated with antibiotics.

5. Herpes is transmitted by vaginal, oral and anal intercourse, and characterised by itching and painful sores. There is no cure, but symptoms can be relieved.

6. Thrush is a yeast in the vagina. Thrush is not necessarily sexually transmitted – it commonly occurs when you take antibiotics – so if you get VD you can often get thrush temporarily from the treatment. It also often occurs when you are run down, upset or eating badly. Thrush is characterised by severe itching and soreness round the labia, and sometimes a thick white discharge. It is painful but does not cause internal damage. Many women have thrush regularly – ways of relieving the symptoms include vinegar douches and inserting yoghurt in the vagina. Doctors prescribe pessaries and sometimes cream to put around the vulva (Nystatin/Nystan or Canesten).

7. *Vaginitis, cystitis* are other infections which you might get from being raped but which are not necessarily sexually transmitted. They are often brought on by emotional stress, and though painful and distressing, do not cause internal damage.

8. *Crabs, scabies, genital warts* can all be caught from physical contact with an infected person, not necessarily sexual. Warts are best treated at a special clinic, but crabs and scabies are treated with Quellada, which you can buy at a chemist. It is also used for head lice.

Medical attitudes and practice

In this section we describe some of the problems experienced by many women in contact with the medical profession after being raped. The practices and attitudes we describe are again British ones, but most apply throughout the English-speaking Commonwealth as well. Doctors can play an important part in helping us take back control of our lives by giving us full and clear information and facilitating our choices, for example, over abortion. Some do so – we are concerned, however, that a great many do not and we concentrate here on these as part of breaking the silence and isolation around the negative experiences many women suffer.

GPs
If you go to your GP and say that you have been raped, you should of course be believed and treated seriously. If there is a possibility of pregnancy, you should be offered information and help about post-

coital contraception, pregnancy tests, abortion, and so on. Many women however meet with scepticism and/or moral judgments which are extremely distressing.

GPs will sometimes ask you whether you have reported to the police, and are more likely to believe you if you have. With some GPs though, you cannot win either way, as if you have reported they may be reluctant to examine you for fear of getting caught up in the legal process and having to give evidence in court. If you do see a doctor who does not believe you, try and be aware of what goes down in your medical records, for example, 'fantasies about rape'. These stay with you for life and you do not have access to them to make changes.

Hospitals/Casualty departments
Hospitals are not under any legal obligation to report to the police that a woman has been raped. However, many hospitals automatically do so when they know a crime has been committed, whether you want them to or not. This depends very much on the sister or doctor in charge of casualty – if you do not want the police brought in, it is worth asking them not to report. If you insist on this though, they will sometimes refuse you treatment. If someone can ring round hospitals for you and ask in advance that they do not report, you may be able to go to one where the doctor will respect your wishes. But that takes time and if it is an emergency may not be possible.

It is outrageous both that hospitals report to the police against women's expressed wishes, and that they pressurise women into agreeing by refusing treatment or in any other way.

Post-coital contraception
Women who are worried about pregnancy are often regarded as irresponsible for having 'unprotected sex', and are encouraged not to be so silly again and to take precautions in the future. Because of this attitude, doctors will sometimes wish to discuss future contraception when you request post-coital contraception – this is utterly inappropriate after a rape, and can be very distressing. Similarly if you have a post-coital IUD inserted and want it removed when you return for a check-up, you may meet with resistance for this reason.

Not many GP s yet provide post-coital contraception – while we would like to see all GP s willing to do so, it is equally important that those who do discuss fully the medical implications with women.

Abortion

The most common problem we meet when requesting an abortion after rape is disbelief. Many GPs, hospital doctors and nurses are, if anything, even more inclined than the rest of society to think that we are lying when we say we have been raped. That women 'cry rape' to get an abortion is a horrifyingly common medical myth. While doctors have the power to grant or not our request for an abortion, many will continue to abuse it with such false judgments. It is worth finding out the names of GPs and gynaecologists who are sympathetic to women wanting abortions – your local rape crisis centre or women's centre should be able to help.

If you get an abortion on the NHS , there is a possibility that you will be put in a maternity or gynaecology ward with women who have had miscarriages, for instance, and may encounter some hostility from staff and patients.

VD clinics

Many VD clinic doctors do make efforts to overcome the associated shame and embarrassment we often feel around VD. They should extend this concern further to women who have been raped and refrain from passing any moral judgments on what has happened. It is not uncommon for doctors to question women in quite unnecessary detail about the circumstances of the rape, and then turn around and blame us for what happened. The doctor's job is medical treatment, not moralist or judge and jury.

You do not have to say more than you wish to about the rape, beyond what is relevant to treatment – doctors should respect your choice. Some, who genuinely want to provide further help, give information about a local RCC where you will get non-judgmental support.

Many of us want to be examined by women doctors – clinics should make this possible in all circumstances but especially after rape, when to be internally examined by a male doctor can feel like another assault. It is worth checking before you go when a woman doctor is available. Doctors are often unaware of the trauma of an internal examination after a rape. They should take special care, and also refrain from unnecessary questions about 'sexual partners'.

VD clinics frequently see girls under 16 with infections, but rarely suspect the possibility of sexual abuse going on either within or outside the family. Doctors should be aware that this is highly likely, that no one else may be in a similar position to suspect it, and should offer girls the opportunity to speak about it, either at the clinic or by giving information about RCC s (see Chapter 7 for more on sexual abuse of girls).

Medical complaints

If any doctors – at police stations, casualty wards, clinics, GP's surgery, or wherever – do not believe you when you tell them you have been raped, make offensive remarks or breach confidentiality about what you tell them, or do anything else which you feel unhappy about, you may wish to consider registering a complaint.

As with all complaints against professionals, they are usually investigated by others in the profession, usually colleagues, and are generally fairly ineffective. Doctors can be prevented from practising for 'serious professional misconduct' but this is rare, and happens only in extreme cases such as alcoholism, sexually assaulting patients, and so on. More likely you will receive a letter of apology, and the doctor concerned will get a 'warning' letter.

There are various different procedures depending on whom you want to complain about and why. You should make your complaint in writing and keep a copy. The time limit for complaining varies, and you should check the full procedure with the appropriate organ-isation or get further information and advice from your local Community Health Council (under Community in phone directories) or Citizens' Advice Bureau, or from the Patients Association (11 Dartmouth Street, London SW1H 9BH; tel: 01-222 4992).

Briefly, the bodies concerned are:

(a) for complaints about forensic doctors, the Association of Police Surgeons;

(b) for complaints about GPs' services, your local Family Practitioner Committee;

(c) for complaints about the professional conduct of GPs or hospital doctors, the General Medical Council (44 Hallam Street, London W1; tel: 01-580 7642);

(d) for complaints about hospital services, the person involved, a senior member of staff or the hospital or district administrator;

(e) for complaints about clinical judgment in hospitals, the consultant in charge of your case or the health authority.

None of these procedures involve financial compensation. This is awarded only for damage to a patient as a result of professional negligence, which must be proved in court.

Apart from the official channels above, if you have a local women's centre or rape crisis centre, you can let them know if you have been badly (or well) treated by a GP so that other women can make better informed choices about whom to register with.

Further reading

Boston Women's Health Book Collective, *Our Bodies Ourselves; a health book by and for women*; British edition by Angela Phillips and Jill Rakusen, Penguin, Harmondsworth, 1980.

Cynthia Cooke and Susan Dworkin, *The Good Health Guide for Women*, originally published in the USA as *The Ms Guide to a Woman's Health*; British edition by Jill Turner and Wendy Savage, Hamlyn, London, 1981.

Federation of Feminist Women's Health Centres, *How to stay out of the Gynaecologist's Office*, Peace Press, California, 1981.

Federation of Feminist Women's Health Centres, *A New View of a Woman's Body*, Touchstone Books, Simon & Shuster, New York, 1981.

If you have difficulty obtaining any of these books, Sisterwrite bookshop (190 Upper St., London N1; tel: 01-226 9782) stocks them all.

7
Sexual Assault of Girls

This chapter is addressed to adult women. It is addressed to any woman who has any contact with or responsibility for any girl, or any woman who has herself been sexually assaulted when young. By speaking to adult women and not to girls exclusively we are recognising that girls are not powerful in our society. They are dependent on adults for the means to stay alive, as well as for protection. In the last few years with the advent of the Women's Liberation Movement and of structures within which women can talk to each other about our experiences, we have been able to speak out about rape. There is much work still to be done, but at least we have a voice. For girls there is no such forum. Adult men are all-powerful to girls. Girls are brought up to obey adults and men stop girls talking about sexual assaults in lots of ways. They do not have the words to describe such assaults and even if they do try to speak about them they are not believed, or told it is not serious. We as adult women must speak on behalf of girls. We must remember what has happened to us in our childhood and speak about it – painful though it may be. We must recognise that girls today are undergoing the same sexual assaults that we underwent and we must try to stop it.

Like rape, the sexual assault of girls is an unrecognised crime: girls are said to have 'asked for it', 'consented to it', 'enjoyed it'. Equally, girls are thought to be lying when they do report this particular crime to the authorities. As with rape, we are told that the men who actually are convicted of committing sexual assault against a girl are not 'normal' – therefore that there are very few of them. When a girl is sexually assaulted by a member of her family she is afforded virtually no protection by society. The rights of the father are paramount in our society and it takes a lot to challenge them.

We know, in fact, from talking to each other and from listening to the women who call the London RCC , that men who sexually assault girls are 'normal' – they come from all races, all classes, and can be of any age.

Girls are made, by an intricate series of myths and by the consequent behaviour of adults, to feel responsible for sexual assaults committed against them. In this section we will examine some of the myths, state the reality, and put the responsibility for sexually assaulting on to the men who commit the crime, not on the children they commit it against.

As with rape, we are forced to use a vocabulary and language that is essentially male-orientated and obscures much of the meaning of sexual assault. We can, however, be clear about what we mean by the words we use. For example, the term 'sexual abuse of children', so commonly used to describe the sexual assault of girls, obscures two realities. The first is that 'children' really means 'girls'. Studies have consistently shown that far more girls are sexually assaulted than boys and the vast majority of the 'abusers' are men. For example, the children's division of the American Humane Association, in a major study found that 92 percent of the children sexually assaulted are girls and that 97 percent of the assailants are adult heterosexual men. The second word in that phrase which carries with it misconceptions is the word 'abuse'. Children do not exist to be used or abused by adults; the word 'abuse' obscures the fact that we are talking about criminal assault. It denies the violence and humiliation of the girls who are assaulted and the seriousness of the crime. We have therefore decided to use the term 'sexual assault of girls'.

Definitions
Defining the sexual assault of girls is not easy. The legal definitions of the crime are set out on pages 27–29. However, legal definitions, while useful if you are dealing with the legal system, are made by men who have no conception of what it feels like to be sexually assaulted. They are therefore of little use in helping us to understand what happens to girls, and are even less use in providing girls with a

vocabulary to help them describe the crime when it is committed against them.

Sexual assault of girls covers a whole range of crimes. It may involve exhibitionism, touching or manipulating the girl's genitals, and getting her to touch a man's genitals, through to oral, anal and vaginal rape. It may involve one or more of these acts. It may occur once or be repeated over a number of months or years.

In our definition of the sexual assault of girls we seldom use the word 'incest'. This is because separating off incest from other sorts of sexual assault of women and girls blurs the fact that the location of power in men/fathers allows them to abuse women and girls in all situations, whether within or outside the family. It is also a term which implies mutuality and participation, and responsibility on the part of the girl being assaulted. Girls do not have the power to refuse or question what adults do.

Incest also has a very specific meaning in law. It only covers sexual intercourse (vaginal rape), when in fact many other forms of assault are involved, and it is an offence only when the woman or girl assaulted is known by the assailant to be his grand-daughter, daughter, sister or mother. It does not include assaults by stepfathers, adoptive fathers, uncles or any other relative.

Who are the Assailants?

As we have already said, it is almost exclusively men who sexually assault girls. Twenty-five percent of assailants are men not known to the girl – strangers.[1] The other 75 percent are known to the girl and are in a position of trust and authority over her. So the myth of the 'dirty old man' in a plastic raincoat is statistically proven wrong. In fact assailants can be fathers, grandfathers, brothers, uncles, neighbours, friends of parents, babysitters, bus drivers, teachers, lodgers, etc., etc. The list is endless – as is the list of 'types' of men who rape women. In other words, any man who has access to any girl is capable of sexually assaulting her, and often does. Since most of the men who do this are in a position of trust over the girls they sexually assault, they are in a position to do great physical and emotional damage to girls with impunity.

Men who rape girls are not perverted, they are normal heterosexual males who have access to girls and choose to use them for their own sexual gratification.

Where does it happen?

In our society we have a propensity to attribute anything 'distasteful' like sexual assault of girls to 'other countries', 'other societies', 'other classes', 'overcrowded families', 'other cultures'. In fact we are willing to look anywhere else but at ourselves, and the men we trust with the care of our children. Sexual assault of girls is common in our society – it happens all the time. It happens in all places where men have access to girls.

Why does it happen?

What makes adult men sexually assault girls? It is not that they are 'mad' (Home Office statistics on convicted rapists show only 2 percent referred for psychiatric treatment). It is rather that they are 'normal'. In our male supremacist society male sexuality is seen to be aggressive – men take the initiative sexually and choose their 'prey' – women. Girls are young women and boys are young men. Boys sexually assault girls as part of normal behaviour. We all know about 'games' in the school bicycle yard – or in the pram sheds of the tower blocks. 'Games' which normally involve groups of boys sexually assaulting smaller groups of girls. Girls find these games at best embarrassing and humiliating – at worst they are destroyed by them. When boys grow up to be men, they do not change their ideas that women and girls are there for their sexual gratification. If they use women as sexual prey (chick, bird, and so on) then they certainly are not going to put an age limit on their prey – in fact many men feel that the younger their 'prey', the better.

It is no wonder, therefore, that the sexual assaults systematically carried out against girls are normally not talked about, are certainly not stopped. Nor is it surprising that almost every adult woman can remember some kind of sexual assault (or series of assaults) that happened to her as a girl. Such assaults are 'normal' – most are not even named as assaults (see Chapter 3 for legal definitions of sexual assault).

Girls are taught from a very young age that the way to earn approval from men (who are very powerful in girls' lives) is to be 'pretty' and 'pleasing'. The way to please is to make themselves sexually accessible to men – to allow them to touch, talk about, and enjoy their bodies. Girls are not allowed to control their bodies and their sexuality and once they have accepted this, they are perfectly prepared for their future roles as wives and mothers and sex objects. By the time we are adult women we may have stopped questioning, we don't even know that the questions exist because we have never been allowed to own our bodies, our sexuality.

When women speak together of our experiences of sexual assault as children we realise that we have *all* been assaulted in one way or another. Whether we have seen the 'local school flasher', been attacked by groups of older boys and made to perform sexual acts for their gratification, been 'touched up' on public transport, been made to kiss uncles or friends of our parents, when unwilling to do so, been made to sit on adult men's knees, been leered at, whistled at, molested or raped.

When does it happen?

Girls of all ages are sexually assaulted. Legal definitions of sexual assault include touching or manipulating a girl's genitals, or making her touch his, through to sexual intercourse (rape).

Like all men who rape women, men who sexually assault girls do not do so out of some sudden uncontrollable sexual desire. They plan in advance what they are going to do, and when the opportunity arises they carry out their plan. They normally do it while the girl's mother is away, say in hospital, or on shift work, while they are left in sole care of the girl. Most sexual assaults are not one-off surprise acts. They are normally carefully prepared and go on for quite a long period of time. So a man might well start by teaching a girl that they have 'secrets' between them that must be kept – then begin 'trading' by giving the girl a toy, sweet or treat of some sort in return for her acquiescence to his handling her body for his gratification. As time goes on he has her trapped, since because she has not spoken about what has been happening with anyone before, he (and society at large) can accuse her of 'colluding', or assume shc is 'consenting'. He is then free to have sexual intercourse with her, for as long as she is unable to speak, or as long as she is not heard.

Of course, most of us know via the media about children who are abducted on their way to school or coming home from the sweet shop and then brutally assaulted and/or murdered. These attacks are an extreme of a continuum of sexual assaults – although they are often presented as the only type of sexual assault which exists.

The question of 'consent'

Over the last decade there has been a growing and sinister trend, on both sides of the Atlantic, to make the overt sexual assault of girls by adult males socially acceptable. It is a campaign which has taken different forms and appeared in different guises, according to the orientation of the campaigners. Its allies range from academic psychologists in pursuit of 'new areas of research' through to peddlers of soft porn eager now to sell legally not only women's but children's bodies for profit. The argument used by the advocates of the legalis-ation of sexual assault on girls is that girls have their own sexuality which they are aware of and in control of, and can (and should have the opportunity to) consent to having a sexual relationship with older men. In order to consent to something, a person must know what it is she is consenting to and she must be free to say yes or no. In our society (or indeed in any society) a young girl does not have the power to say yes or no to an adult man – she is in such a dependent position that she cannot negotiate in that way.

Young girls do not necessarily know what sex actually is. They want to be held, to have love and affection but it is adults who impute a sexual motivation to a girl's sensual activities. If this makes the adults feel sexual it is *they* who choose to act on those feelings, not the girl.

When considering the question of consent, we as adult women cannot separate ourselves off from children and young women. As we grow older we may begin to know what it is we are consenting to, but are we really free to consent to having a sexual relationship with a man in a society where we do not hold equal power with men? Do we really have a choice when we (and they) know that if we say 'no' they can rape us with impunity? Married women, for example, do not have the legal right to say no to sexual intercourse with their husbands, because men cannot be charged with raping their wives.

Under the present law, it is a crime for adult men to have sexual intercourse with children, and if it is proved that a man has had sex with a girl under the age of 16 (the legal age of consent) then his guilt is automatically proven. There is pressure from many groups for the legal age of consent to be lowered – or even abolished. If this happened, then a girl who was sexually assaulted or raped would be placed in the same position as that of an adult woman who had been raped, namely that she would be required to prove that she did not consent. It would, in effect, finally shift the legal (as well as moral) responsibility from men who sexually assault girls on to the girls themselves.

The sexual assault of girls within the family
The nature of male power in families means that there is always a possibility of sexual assault on any girl, because men and society regard families as places in which men do what they choose. The girls it happens to are not any different from those who are not assaulted – rather some escape because the men who are our fathers, guardians or friends chose not to abuse their power. Men see 'their' children as belonging to them – not primarily as individuals with feelings and needs and rights but as servicers of their emotional, sexual and domestic needs.

Writers and practitioners working on sexual assault of girls continue to elaborate a mythology which is extremely effective in perpetuating sexual assaults on girls within the family. The most popular version is related to 'family dysfunction'. This is intended to put blame and responsibility for sexual assaults on anyone other than the man who commits the crime. Although they are careful to say they do not condone the offender's behaviour, they justify it by saying that the blame lies within all the family. It comes as no surprise to us to learn that they see it lying with the 'colluding' mother or the 'provocative' daughter.

Protecting girls from sexual assault

As women we have little power in this society. However, that does not mean that we cannot go some way towards protecting girls from sexual assault. It is important when reading this section to remember that if a child for whom you have responsibility is sexually assaulted, it is *not* your fault – nor is it hers. You have not assaulted her and cannot be expected to be present every time she is left alone with a man.

The first thing we can do as adult women is realise that any man, no matter how much you trust him, is capable of sexually assaulting a girl. We cannot distinguish between men who are 'safe' and men who are not 'safe'. This awareness enables us to listen when girls try to tell us that they are being sexually assaulted. For example, if a girl is uncomfortable with a particular male babysitter, or if she does not like being left alone with her father, brother, uncle or friend of the family – or any adult man – then it is important to find out why, painful though it may be. He may well be sexually assaulting her. Equally, if you feel funny about any man being left with a girl, if he speaks or acts in a way that makes you feel suspicious, it is important to listen to your own feelings and find out what is happening. Normally, our suspicions are based on concrete things and dismissing them as a 'paranoia' or 'neurosis' may well result in a girl being very badly hurt. It is important to think carefully about leaving girls alone with men, whether members of the family or professionals – especially if they show any uneasiness about being with them.

There are some specific recognisable signals which might well indicate that a girl is being sexually assaulted. If you notice that:

(a) If an adult man shows disrespect for a girl's requests through repeated patting, tickling or repeated attempts at physical contact with her when she clearly does not want such contact, then he clearly does not recognise her rights to set limits on physical contact.

(b) Adults who like children often invite them into their homes. If an adult man consistently does this to a girl then it is worth checking on what happens when she is there.

(c) Any man who relates to a girl in a sexual manner – saying things like 'she's a charmer', or 'she's sexy' – may be dangerous. Even if he does not actually physically assault her, for a young girl to work out

such concepts is difficult and she should not have to do so until she is ready.

(d) Men who batter their wives frequently assault their children as well. If they have access to girls they are likely to sexually assault them as well as other children.

(e) Men who say that a particular girl lies a lot, or men who have been previously accused of sexually assaulting a girl are dangerous. Saying that girls are lying when they try to speak about sexual assault is the most frequent response of men who are accused of the crime.

(f) Men who share secrets with girls should be stopped from this practice. It is unfair on any child to expect it to keep a secret with one adult from another. It is by engendering such secrets that men gain continued access to girls, and can continue to sexually assault them, sometimes for years.

Teaching girls to protect themselves

It is important that we teach girls to protect themselves from sexual assault, *without* making them feel responsible for the crime if it happens to them. Telling girls not to accept gifts from strangers, not to speak to or get into cars with strange men will not necessarily protect from sexual assault. If girls do accept sweets etc., they are *not* responsible for being raped. Young children are taught to trust and are easily tricked by adult men who abuse that trust.

Furthermore, it is not only strangers that girls must be aware of. Eighty-five percent of men who sexually assault girls are known to them and their families. We should allow girls the right to refuse to be touched, and back up that right when it is being abused by adults. In family social situations, for example, a girl should not be encouraged to go round the room kissing all her relatives if she does not want to.

Another effective tool we can give girls to protect themselves from men is our belief. If a girl is sure she will be believed and that she will not be punished if she is sexually assaulted, she may well be able to speak about a situation that is developing into sexual assault. If you believe her, and stop it, she will be far more sure about herself and much more secure in her knowledge of her own self-worth than she would have been had you not believed her and acted.

We can give girls some power to say 'no', by teaching them to say to anyone who wishes them to do something they do not feel comfortable with that they have to ask our permission first. In that way they are protected and assured of our support.

How girls react to sexual assault

This section is not intended to prescribe how girls should react to being sexually assaulted. What we intend in writing it is that adult women should recognise some of the things that girls tell them about sexual assault. Many girls are unable to describe with words what has happened, but their behaviour indicates clearly that they have been sexually assaulted. In writing about some of the more common reactions, we would also like to reassure adult women who know girls who have been sexually assaulted that they (the girls) do not necessarily need any kind of psychiatric treatment – but that their reactions are 'normal'.

Sudden change in attitude towards an adult man
Girls who are sexually assaulted may suddenly decide, quite rightly, that they do not like a particular man with whom they are in contact. They may also become fearful of any man, not wanting to touch or be touched. There is nothing wrong with this, and it is in fact a very healthy sign of self-protection. Sexual assualts are not normally one-off – they normally last over a period of time. The adult man, if he is not already trusted by the girl, normally tries to build up as much trust as possible before assaulting her. This way he is less likely to be found out, because she will be confused about what is happening and may be open to having 'secrets' which can't be spoken about. If a girl can withstand that kind of pressure and actually say that she does not like the man then that is a very good thing. Equally, if a girl suddenly becomes reluctant to use a favourite play place, then it is not necessarily that she is being difficult – she may have been assaulted there.

Expressing affection in inappropriate ways
If a girl expresses affection in ways which are overtly sexual, for example 'french kissing' or offering to take her clothes off for men she

likes, then it is quite likely that she has been sexually assaulted. Girls do not learn such behaviour alone (or instinctively).

Sleep problems

Nightmares, bedwetting (especially if it starts suddenly), trouble falling asleep, suddenly needing a light on at night are very common reactions to being sexually assaulted. In fact, not only young girls have these problems, adult women often have difficulty with sleep patterns after being raped. Obviously, the above sleep disturbances happen to children for all kinds of reasons. Normally, however, sexual assault is overlooked as one of the causes of these, whereas it should be seen as very probable.

Sudden behaviour changes

After being sexually assaulted, girls often undergo radical behaviour changes. A very outgoing girl may become very withdrawn, and vice versa. An inability to concentrate in school, a falling off of academic standard, loss of appetite or sudden increase of appetite – all of these can happen after a sexual assault (or during a series of assaults). These are ways of indicating that something traumatic has happened, and that the girl is out of control of her behaviour.

'Blocking'

Blocking is something that many women and girls do in order to cope with being raped or sexually assaulted. It means that the assault or series of assaults is put out of your mind to the extent that you do not actually remember that anything has happened – you just have blank spots in your memory. Girls especially block the experience of assault because they do not have the opportunity to talk about it, and usually feel guilty and bad, and fear some terrible punishment. Men are clever at playing on this fear in order to ensure a girl's silence.

This blocking results in a girl being able to live an apparently 'normal' life – never speaking about the assault.

Many women are suddenly reminded as adults about a sexual assault which happened in childhood, and when this happens it is a very real shock. For example, talking about sexual assault, seeing a television programme, going to therapy, reading a book such as this one can suddenly bring back the memory of a terrible experience. If this happens it is a good idea to try to talk about it. It may seem unreal, you may think it is just your overactive imagination. We rarely imagine such assaults. By talking about it you may be able to gain control over the feelings of powerlessness that the memory brings. It is possible to verify such assaults by asking mothers or sisters or aunts. Confronting the man who assaulted you is usually difficult – they usually deny the incident(s) completely, leaving you with a disturbing sense of unreality.

Becoming pregnant as an adult woman can also remind you of a previous sexual assault. When women are pregnant, we are out of control of our bodies, which grow to look different. We are also out of control of the changes in the ways other people perceive us. Equally, having an abortion can remind you of being sexually assaulted. Many women, when raped as adults, are devastated by the memory it brings of previous assaults. All the feelings we described above may come up at any time.

Adult women

Many adult women who have experienced overt and sustained sexual assault as girls, find that the pain and the feeling of being out of control of your sexuality stays with you. It often feels bound up with a lack of trust in men. In fact it is more likely that you control your sexuality more tightly than women who were not taught so clearly as girls that men abuse our sexuality. Not trusting men is actually not harmful – but is a realistic way of protecting yourself. If as a child you learn that adult men are not to be trusted, then that is not false – they are not to be trusted. Many women know this but take some time to act on it.

Mothers and blaming them

A lot of anger is often directed at mothers by women who have been raped as girls – especially if the man who assaulted you was your father. Children believe that adults are all-powerful, and often believe that mothers are the main protectors. In our society mothers are seen as being responsible for everything that happens to a child – whatever it is. While mothers do have a responsibility to protect girls

– so do social services, the teaching profession, the police force and neighbours. It is only possible to protect a girl to a certain extent; after that men must take responsibility not to commit these crimes against girls.

Mothers are held responsible for sexual assaults on girls by trusted men in authority, on two counts. One argument is that there is an impaired sexual relationship which creates unrelieved sexual tension in their husbands or male cohabitees who are then 'forced' by their 'uncontrollable sexual urges' to rape their daughters. This is rubbish and nothing more than a continuation of the idea that women and girls exist for men's sexual gratification. Secondly, they argue that the mother always knows that her daughter is being sexually assaulted (consciously or unconsciously – you can't win). And she, not the man, is held responsible for not protecting her daughter. Mothers, as well as many other women involved with girls, need to think about and try to stop sexual assault – *but we do not commit the crime* – it is for men to stop assaulting girls.

Guilt

As with rape, girls who are sexually assaulted are invariably made to feel guilty for what has happened – by family, friends, the man who sexually assaulted her and society generally. Unless a girl is taken away by a strange man when she is doing something that she has been given permission to do, she will be blamed by those charged with her care for what has happened. Even if she is not blamed by others, most girls (like adult women) look to their own behaviour to find the reason for the attack. Girls often carry this guilt with them throughout their lives.

For adult women who have contact with or responsibility for girls who are actually sexually assaulted

If a child in your care, or whom you know, has been sexually assaulted you may be very upset. It may remind you of something that happened to you as a girl, you may feel guilty for not knowing it was going to happen and for not protecting her. You may be hurt that someone has hurt a girl you love. If the man who has assaulted the girl is a friend, relation, boyfriend or husband of yours then you may be confused about whether to believe the man (who will almost certainly deny it) or the girl. Whether or not to act, what to do that is best for the girl? The action you decide to take will probably depend on the situation. However, your reaction to the girl who has told you that she has been sexually assaulted is crucial for her well-being. Below are some guidelines we think are important. We got this information by remembering ourselves how we would have liked adults to react to us as girls, and by listening to the hundreds of adult women who have come to the London Rape Crisis Centre and talked about what had hurt them in adult reactions to sexual assaults against them as girls.

The most important thing is *belief*. Girls need to be assured that they do not have to 'prove' a sexual assault – that they have your belief and your support. In short, that you are on their side.

As well as belief, girls need to know that they have not done anything wrong, and that they will not be punished for what has happened to them. They need to know that the man who sexually assaulted them is definitely wrong and should be punished. It is important that you *tell* them this. You may well feel very angry about what has been done to a girl – most of us do when we hear of sexual assaults against girls. It is important, if you are angry, to assure the girl that you are not angry at her, but at the man who did it.

It is a bad idea to start rushing into action as soon as a girl lets you know that she has been sexually assaulted. More often than not the assaults will have been going on for some time. Try to find out gently what happened – but it is important not to force girls to say what happened if they don't want to. They will tell you in their own time and this is one area where a child can and should be allowed to take control. This will be the beginning of her learning to control her life, and to deal with the feelings of powerlessness generated by such sexual assaults.

Once you have provided caring and support, and have found out what happened, it is then possible to decide rationally how best to act in the interests of the girl. It is important here to remember that neither the girl nor you have a 'duty' to society to stop rape. The only people with that responsibility are the men who commit the crime. Your primary concern should be the girl's welfare. It is important that she is given some control over whatever action you take (or do not take), without leaving her with the responsibility of making major decisions that she is not ready or able to make.

Your anger might well lead you into thinking that the man must be caught and punished. It is true that he should be, but not necessarily true that he will be. So you need to think about going to the police – especially if it was a stranger who sexually assaulted the girl.

The police

The procedure for reporting a sexual assault on a girl is almost exactly the same as reporting a rape (see Chapter 4). The same myths apply – that girls ask for, or are lying about the offence (unless it is medically very obvious that a girl has been sexually assaulted). No girl under 16 should be questioned or medically examined without a parent or guardian with her. If a member of the family (especially the father) has sexually assaulted the girl then it is usually more difficult to get the police to act. Firstly, there must be forensic evidence that sexual intercourse has taken place between the girl and her father and secondly, the police appear to have a policy, especially if a girl is young, of not charging men who deny the offence against their daughters. It seems that the police force thinks it is too traumatic for a child to go through the court process and men are often let off with a warning. In this way the girls are left unprotected in families where they are being raped and sexually assaulted.

Being taken into care

If it is a member of the family who is sexually assaulting the girl, especially if it is her father, and he is not charged with the offence, the Local Authority may be informed. Sometimes the police do this, sometimes other adults who know what is happening. By and large Local Authorities are reluctant to take action which may 'split up the family'. However, they do have the power to take girls into care and sometimes they exercise that power. If a girl is taken into care and her father is left at home she may feel that she is being punished and that therefore she has done something wrong. She should be reassured clearly that she is not to blame and is in care for her protection. It must be remembered that the relative 'safety' of being in local author-ity care may be a relief to a girl who has been living with a man who is sexually assaulting her.

Court

Again, the court procedure is the same for girls and adult women who report sexual offences (see Chapter 5). The only difference here is that where girls under 16 are concerned the case is usually heard 'in camera'. This means that the public are not allowed into the courtroom. The press normally attend such hearings but if they report on them they are not allowed to disclose the girl's identity.

Medical

When people think of girls being raped or sexually assaulted they think that they must be very badly injured. While many young girls are injured, more often than not the offender will have had access to the girl over a long period of time and will have prepared her physi-cally to be penetrated. Therefore she might not appear to be physically injured. This does not in any way mean that she has not been sexually assaulted (see medical chapter for more information).

VD

Girls often get VD from being raped or sexually assaulted. Many very young girls are regularly treated by VD clinics for different types of venereal disease. Contrary to popular mythology, girls do not catch VD from toilet seats, or from being in the vicinity of venereal disease. They catch it, like adult women, through sexual contact usually with adult men. Since a VD clinic is a place where a girl can be medically examined and treated without her parents' consent or knowledge, it would be possible for VD clinics to obtain the necessary evidence that girls are being sexually assaulted to have the assaults stopped. Unfortunately, they choose not to do this and knowingly send girls back into families or situations where this is happening.

After a girl has been raped, it is necessary to be aware of the possibility that she might have caught a venereal disease (see Chapter 6 for more information). Some VD clinics have specialist workers who examine children, some do not. It is worth phoning to check before bringing a child to a particular clinic. Having a VD check-up of course entails having an internal examination. Many girls don't want to have one after being raped. If you both decide that it is better that she does not have a check-up, then you need to be aware that continued stomach pains or abdominal pains or any kind of unusual vaginal discharge indicate that she has caught a venereal disease. It is very important that this be treated medically. As with adult women, girls can be greatly reassured that they are not 'permanently damaged' by the attack.

Pregnancy

See Chapter 6 for information on pregnancy tests, abortion, and so on. Girls under 16 usually find it very difficult to obtain pregnancy tests and especially abortion without the consent of their parent or guardian.

How girls are after it has happened

As with adult women, the length of time it takes a girl to 'recover' after being raped depends on the circumstances of the offence. How long it went on for before she said anything about it, whether the man who sexually assaulted her was trusted or not, and what he said to her, are all factors. It also depends on how those around her react to the fact that she has been sexually assaulted.

The most important thing therefore is that a girl is offered comfort, support and belief once she has spoken of being assaulted – as well as clear protection from the offender.

Talking   Many adults wonder whether or not to encourage a girl to talk about a rape. Girls, like adult women, can benefit from sharing it. Talking helps them to gain control and understanding of what has happened. Girls can express themselves in words, or with drawings or dolls – it is very important that they be allowed to do so and that the adults they tell are not embarrassed, punishing or disbelieving.

It is possible for adults close to girls to bring the assaults up in conversation by recognising what a girl is indicating. For example, if the man is known to her and she sees him or mentions him then you can ask her how she feels about him now. Like adult women, girls must choose their time to talk, and should not be forced to do so.

Nightmares   If a girl is having nightmares or her sleep is being disturbed then it is a good idea to allow her to speak about them if she can. Even if she does not want to, or cannot tell you what the nightmares are about, you can assure her that she is protected and that you will look after her.

Questions   Girls are sometimes concerned about what will happen to the man – especially if he was known to her. It is usually impossible for you to say, especially if the matter has been reported to the police. It is important to let a child know this and to find out what prompted the question. It is also important to let the girl know that she is not responsible for what will happen to him.

'Getting back to normal'   The sooner a girl resumes a normal pattern of life after being sexually assaulted the better. However, how soon she will be able to do this depends on the circumstances of the assault. For example, if it was her father who was raping her then she and her mother might have to change homes, and she may have to go to a different school. As with talking, she can be encouraged but not forced to do 'normal' things like going regularly to school, and so on. These will give her a sense of security and some reassurance that her life will not be disrupted for ever.

Girls do not just get gradually 'better' after being sexually assaulted. A child may seem to be back to "normal" and then will have setbacks where she starts having nightmares or refuses to leave her home or mother. However, she may gradually have less night-mares – they may stop altogether and they may not. Once a girl is able to play comfortably with friends, is willing to risk new situations and able to express anger or assert her will, she is well on the way to *controlling her own life.*

Psychotherapy – 'treatment' Many people feel that girls need 'treatment' after being raped or sexually assaulted. As with adult women, girls who are sexually assaulted are not 'ill' and do not need treatment. However, sometimes girls find it impossible to talk to parents or adults close to them after being raped, for all kinds of reasons. If this is the case it may be worth offering the girl someone whom she does not know (but who will be sympathetic) to talk to. It is important to know what the person she talks to thinks about rape. Many therapists believe that girls secretly want to be raped and unconsciously provoke it. Such attitudes do far more harm than good. You, as the person responsible for the girl, will have a lot of pressure on you to deal effectively with what has happened. It is important that you recognise your own need for support. Sometimes family and friends can be helpful. Sometimes it is more appropriate to contact an outside agency such as a rape crisis centre.

Taking action to stop the sexual assault of girls

See Chapter 9 for 'taking action to stop rape'. There are things you can do as an individual and within your community.

(a) Talk about it. It is the silence which surrounds the sexual assault of girls, within and outside the family, which allows it to continue unchecked in our society. When, for example, you hear jokes told about it you could make it clear that sexually assaulting young girls is not funny and that they do not 'enjoy it'.

(b) Act when you know it is happening. Professionals particularly are very adept at ignoring sexual assault, particularly when it happens within a family. It is not better for a child to *stay* in a family where she is being sexually assaulted than *to go into care.* Professionals such as social workers, teachers and doctors, who know what is happening to a girl and who make no attempt to recognise or stop what is happen-ing, are colluding with the offender in what he is doing. If you are

suspicious that a man you know is sexually assaulting a girl you know then it is probably happening. It is worth actually finding out whether it is or not, rather than deciding that suspicions are unjustified.

(c) Community action. 'Flashers', for example, are not funny and are not harmless. They are frightening and dangerous. It is important that local communities pressurise police and court systems to act when they know these men are around and to charge and punish them. Also, pressure must be put on our legal system so that it becomes easier for girls to report sexual assaults and for the police to act on those reports.

(d) Schools. Girls in school should be taught about the possibility of sexual assault and what to do if it happens. So few schools have anything about rape or sexual assault on their curriculums and it is something that *is likely to happen to a great number of the pupils.*

Text of a leaflet available from the London Rape Crisis Centre

Your body is your own – no man or boy should touch you in a way you don't like.
Rape is being forced by a man to have sex with him.
Sexual assault is being touched by or made to touch a man in a way you don't like.

A man touching you with his hands, rubbing against you with his body or kissing you in a way that makes you feel scared, hurt or funny is wrong and he knows this.

If he asks you to take your clothes off even if he says it is a game or a punishment and you feel funny, he is wrong.

Men or boys should not do this to girls.
If it does happen, it is not a girl's fault. Nobody, not even your parents, has the right to do anything sexual to you that you don't understand or want. It is all right to want it to stop.

The men or boys who do this to girls can be men you don't know. They can also be part of your family, like fathers, uncles, brothers,

grandfathers, stepfathers: they can be teachers, social workers, doctors, friends or babysitters: they can be neighbours or boys in the playground.

Men or boys can sexually assault girls at any time.

A man may be doing this to you now or you may have been assaulted some time ago. You may not have been sure what was going on. Maybe you were so scared that you forgot about it, you may have bad dreams, you may not like to be alone with a man or boy.

If you are being sexually assaulted you may feel scared or worried. It may be hard but it helps to tell somebody about it.

Who can you tell?

Think of all the people you know. Pick someone who is kind and who you can trust. This can be your mother; it may seem hard to tell her but she can be a good friend.

If your mother is not the best person perhaps you can tell a teacher, an aunt, a sister, a neighbour or the mother of one of your friends. You may not be believed or understood by the person you tell but keep trying. When you share what has happened with someone else, that gives you the strength of two.

If you are feeling ill or sore after being sexually assaulted you need to see a doctor. It is good to have a grown-up that you trust with you.

What happens if you tell?

The person you tell can help you stop it. They can tell the man to stop sexually assaulting you. They can tell you what will happen if you go to the police or social services. They may go to the police or social services themselves but if you don't want them to do this you can ask them not to. You may not have a choice about what they do. They may not do anything. They may not believe you. If they don't it does not mean it is not happening, or that you are wrong to talk about it and want it stopped.

The police

Reporting rape or sexual assault to the police can be very hard. If they believe you they will ask a lot of questions and want a doctor to examine you. They may not do anything at all. You must have a grown-up with you when you tell the police if you are under 16. It is helpful too if you have to go to court.

If the police are told it could mean that the man who raped or sexually assaulted you may be punished or go to prison. If he does it is *HIS FAULT*, not yours. If the man is your father you may be taken to be looked after by someone else. This is not because you have done anything wrong, it is to protect you from him.

Remember:
Your body is yours and no man or boy should touch it without you saying they can. If they do, you have the right to say no without feeling bad. Any man or boy who rapes or sexually assaults you knows that what he is doing is a crime.

If you have been sexually assaulted or raped, or you have a sister or friend who this has happened to and you don't know what to do – you can ring the London Rape Crisis Centre on 01–837 1600 *at any time, day or night.* We will always believe you and we will not tell anyone about what you tell us.

8
Sexual Harassment at Work

There has recently been some considerable public controversy on this subject, if for no other reason than an apparent difficulty in clearly defining it. Arguments rage both 'for' and 'against' taking it seriously. 'For' – that it is a largely unrecognised but widespread crime against women, a form of discrimination in the workplace; 'against' – that it is part and parcel of 'life' in the office or factory, inevitable in a situation where women and men are obliged to mix, and something which 'the feminists' are trying to blow up out of all proportion.

Sexual harassment can be defined as any unwanted sexual attention in the workplace, from bosses, co-workers, clients, patients, etc., that undermines your confidence in yourself and/or your work; prevents you doing your job properly; creates a stressful work environment; threatens your job security or chances of promotion and therefore your livelihood (and in many cases, prevents you from getting a job in the first place). It can involve touching, pinching, rubbing up against you, actual physical assault or rape, as well as verbal assault – sexual innuendo, jokes, comments on your appearance, sexual propositions and emotional blackmail. In short, any sexual behaviour that makes you feel uncomfortable, embarrassed, compromised or ill at ease.

The effects can be far-ranging: becoming nervous, losing weight, loss of sleep, general 'fretting', withdrawing socially, loss of self-confidence resulting in poor work standards, ending finally in leaving the job, or being effectively forced to resign, or perhaps being moved or sacked as a result of complaining.

It should be made clear that by sexual harassment we are talking specifically about behaviour that is unwanted and uninvited. We are *not* talking about consensual sexual relationships between co-workers. Deliberately confusing the two is a common way by which men prevent the sexual harassment experienced by women from being taken seriously. What we are talking about is the deliberate coercion of women – usually in a subordinate position – by men, using the sexual means described above.

As with rape, many fallacies abound about behaviour of this kind by men towards women, in the workplace. Some are listed below:

(a) Women who object to sexual harassment have no sense of humour. This is a very commonly held view. We are accused of over-reacting to what is supposed to be a bit of harmless fun (fun for whom?). Again as with rape, it is men who commit these acts, and men who define what they are. Behaviour that causes physical symptoms of distress, and often forces women eventually to leave their jobs, is *not* harmless fun.

(b) Women often make false allegations of sexual harassment at work. This belief is held by those with a low opinion of the female sex in general. (The same is often said of allegations of rape; the parallels are obvious.) We all know we face disbelief, hostility and censure when we complain of sexual harassment or assault. This being the case, what is there to be gained by falsehood? The *reality* is that women have a very great deal to lose (job, income, promotion prospects, health, self-respect, respect of colleagues, and so on) and nothing to gain by complaining of sexual harassment without foundation.

(c) 'No' should be enough to stop it. The idea is that any woman ought to be able to state, firmly and categorically, that she does not like what is happening, and that she would like it to stop. Miraculously it is then supposed to stop. But what about that other well-known myth, that 'No' really means 'Yes'? Whichever way we turn we are caught. All the loopholes are tightly closed against us, and against our being allowed to be sexually free and self-determined. Added to which is the issue of power in female–male relationships, of whatever nature. Obviously, if the man harassing you is your boss, or generally in a higher position than you, it is highly unlikely that you

will tell him flatly to go away and leave you alone. To do so you risk losing your job, or your chances of promotion, or both. But even with a colleague of equal ranking, chances are he will rate higher, come the crunch, in the promotion stakes, which makes you more expendable than he is.

Women are usually relatively expendable in paid employment. We are tolerated by the predominantly male workforce – on sufferance in effect – so long as we knuckle under to our given role, and do not rock the boat too much. And what better way to keep us down there in our place, stop us getting too uppity, too ambitious, too much of a risk to male jobs (therefore male power)? By having to face the endless humiliation of jokes, uninvited touching, sexual propositions, by being surrounded by pin-ups of naked women in our workplaces, we are constantly reminded of the way we are viewed, the value we are given, by the male-dominated society in which we live. To pretend that one firm 'No' can change all that, and immediately cause men to stop treating us as bodies and start treating us as equals, is to practise monumental self-delusion.

(d) 'Professional' women do not suffer from sexual harassment. Many people believe that sexual harassment is in effect a working-class problem; that articulate, well-educated, middle-class women do not encounter it. Though women are moving more into managerial positions, they are still in the minority, and the majority will still be subordinate to men. Perhaps the harassment may be slightly more subtle (invitations or orders to spend nights or weekends away with the boss), but it is still there. In fact the risks of career prospects being damaged are greater for some professional women, since their job circles are small, and word travels fast on professional grapevines. So that a woman who is brave enough to make a fuss about being sexually harassed at work is likely to find her reputation (and job prospects elsewhere) considerably soured.

An important element of sexual harassment is the coercive one. Women often find that they are too embarrassed or intimidated to rebuff sexual advances (especially ones from a superior). So that the longer the situation continues, the more difficult it is to halt.

We, as women, are all taught to avoid confrontation. As little boys are taught to be physical and open in their disputes, so we are taught to be meek, submissive and peace-making. So many years of conditioning are hard to break. We continue to hope that by avoiding or ignoring what is happening, matters may resolve themselves or even disappear altogether, without our having to confront the issue (or him).

We are also taught that male attention is flattering, and that we must seek it constantly. We are not taught, however, that it is often far from pleasant – even humiliating and distressing. And of course men cannot be expected to admit that much of their behaviour is clearly and deliberately harassing, and not at all flattering. As with rape, we can be easily sexually harassed because of our vulnerability, and by the knowledge that continual harassment *works*. It does what men intend it to: it demeans and undermines us, saps our strength and self-confidence, and very firmly illustrates who pulls the strings in our society.

How, then, do we handle it? One thing is for sure: ignoring sexual harassment at work will *not* make it go away.

If you work with other women, talk to them about it (it is surprising – and depressing – how much sympathy and shared experience you will find). The more of you there are to complain, the less likely you are to be dismissed as a one-off, humourless, vindictive neurotic, who cannot handle her work relationships.

Keep track – a diary, if necessary – of all incidents of harassment, including your rebuffs, the responses you get, times, dates, and so on. This will help if and when you make a formal complaint.

If you feel unable to make a clear verbal statement to the harasser of your dislike of his behaviour, write it all down and send it to him (keep a copy for yourself). Make it clear that if it does not stop you are prepared to complain to high places. If you have any sympathetic women friends or colleagues, get them to check it over for you. Every little bit of support helps. Make him aware that you are not alone, and that there are others around who know what he is doing, and are watching him. Groups are much more difficult to intimidate and silence than individuals.

If you belong to a union, try and find a woman officer to talk to about it. If there is no union, or one that is unrecognised by management, try and find a woman personnel officer to tell. Given the nature and extent of the problem, and men's unwillingness to admit its prevalence or importance, you are in the main more likely to get somewhere if you complain to a woman.

Below are some broad guidelines for formal complaints. NB : Where possible make complaints *in writing,* and keep copies of all your letters and their responses.

1. Non-union procedure

(a) Complain to, if possible, a *woman* personnel officer;

(b) if not, to your head of department (boss?);

(c) if you got the job through an employment agency, let them know (that they should not deal with clients who harass women).

2. Union procedure

(a) Complain to your Women's Rights Officer, if there is one;

(b) if not, go to your shop steward. If he is the harasser, try your district official;

(c) preferably with some support, pressurise your union to establish a grievance procedure, to be used in all cases (the Transport & General Workers Union (TGWU), for instance, holds that anyone displaying 'gross industrial misconduct' would entitle a company to dismiss that person[1]).

3. Agency workers ('temps')

(a) Complain to the agency first, as your employer.

(b) Do not allow yourself simply to be moved to another job as a solution. Remind them that the same will happen to your successors if nothing is done.

(c) Try and find others who have worked at the same place, who can possibly support you in your complaints.

4. Complaint to the police

You can also consider a formal complaint to the police, either for indecent assault or rape (see Chapter 3, section on charges).

Remember:

● Sexual harassment at work *is* a serious issue (men can *afford* to joke about it).
● To complain about it is not over-reacting; it is perfectly reasonable.
● It does cost women jobs, income, health and peace of mind.
● You have the right to work in an environment that is free from hassle and problems of this kind.
● There is no reason why any woman should have to 'put up with it'.

9
Taking Action

Rape is the responsibility of men, not of women. While men continue to humiliate and control women through our sexuality, we cannot take responsibility for 'prevention'. Whatever action we take or do not take to improve our safety – to survive – if we are raped it is not our responsibility. In discussing here some of the action we can take to protect ourselves, we are *not* saying 'if you do this or don't do that, you won't be raped', nor should women who have been raped look for ways they could have avoided or prevented it. There are no foolproof prescriptions. It is more a question of listening to our fears, recognising that for women living in a male-dominated society they are real and valid, and finding ways to make trusting these feelings constructive, rather than paralysing.

Whether we recognise it or not, all women live with the fear of male violence as part of our everyday lives. We adapt to it in ways that we take for granted and often hardly notice. Most of us, if we are walking down the street alone, will be instantly aware of a man's approach or male footsteps behind us. You may cross the road, go into a shop, or even take care not to walk alone in the first place. You may walk on, apparently unperturbed, but you will not be feeling relaxed any more. If a strange man is in your house, reading the meter, for instance, you will feel safer when he has left. If you find yourself in a lift with a man alone, you may well feel uncomfortable. These feelings are not 'being silly' or 'neurotic' – they are the result of the power relationship between men and women and the way it affects all male—female interactions. Take the meter reader again: if you are friendly and talk to him, society will see that as 'chatting him up', asking to be raped in fact – the courts make a meal of any conversations a woman has had with the rapist. If you do not talk to him, you are being hostile, and risk 'provoking' violence in that way. These examples only deal with strangers of course. When you know too that it is equally possible to be raped by a man you trust, you can no longer see certain men as protectors (against other men) and will lose the illusion of safety that, for example, having your husband or male lover at home with you or walking in the street with you may have given.

Recognising that the threat we live under is due to our status as women, and not to any individual characteristic or weakness, and that so many unnamed fears focus clearly on male violence, can be strengthening. Sharing these everyday fears with other women is an important part of gaining that recognition, and drawing strength from our collective anger at the control men exercise over our lives.

Individual action

Anything you want to do that will make you feel safer is worth doing. Below are some suggestions:

At home   To avoid men knowing that a woman lives at your address, do not put your full name on your doorbell or in the phonebook, just your initials and surname. Get a strong chain or a spyhole on your front door so you can see who is there before opening it, and if a man calls claiming to be a meter reader, plumber, etc. ask for identification before letting him in. Do not be afraid to refuse entry if you are not satisfied. If you find this difficult – as many of us do, brought up as we are to be polite and accommodating – talk with other women about it and practise what you will say. If you think there is someone in your house, breaking a window may attract attention and enable you to get out if possible.

On the street   If you feel afraid walking alone, you could approach another woman walking in the same direction and walk together

Otherwise it is best to walk quickly and purposefully, to keep where possible to well-lit streets and not to stop if men ask you the time or for directions. If you think you are being followed, go into a pub if there is one open and tell the publican or ask to use the phone and call a friend. If it is late and there is nowhere open, but you are in a built-up area, keep walking and make a lot of noise. People are more likely to respond to cries of 'Fire' than 'Help' or 'Rape'. If there are people about, tell the nearest woman what is happening. If you are about to be attacked, run.

On public transport   Try to sit near to another woman if you are travelling alone. On trains or tubes, do not be afraid to pull the emergency cord.

Driving alone   Keeping your doors and windows locked will prevent a man getting in when you are stopped at traffic lights, for instance. If you think you are being followed in a car, drive to the nearest police station. Avoid giving lifts to men, but if you can, pick up women hitching on their own.

Contact with workers in traditionally male professions   If you employ an electrician or plumber or see a doctor, dentist, optician, etc. you can ask to see a woman. If there is one available it is a simple way to feel safer. If there is not, asking will at least increase pressure for more women workers in all fields, and awareness of the threat women suffer in contacts with men.

Self-defence   There has recently been increased interest in self-defence and martial arts and there are now many classes run by women for women. Developing your physical strength and using it to protect yourself in any way is undoubtedly valuable. A word or two of caution though. Self-defence techniques are sometimes misleadingly presented as instant and foolproof remedies for attack. Rape is an act of violence during which control of the situation is completely taken away from the woman – each of us has to judge what we must do to survive. Fear for your life, fear of provoking further violence, shock and disbelief, less physical strength than the attacker and many other factors may influence your response during an attack. While self-defence can teach you effective actions in controlled conditions, in a violent situation only you can judge what you are able to do at that moment to endure and survive what is happening. It is often difficult to remember later the extreme feelings of terror and disbelief that may accompany an attack. If you choose not to fight, it does not mean you consent to rape. This is the other danger of self-defence – that it can become yet another way in which we are forced to assume responsibility for being raped. The myth is perpetuated that rape is part of a natural order against which we as women must be prepared to protect ourselves or be blamed for the consequences.

However, within the context of becoming aware of the reality of male violence, of trusting our feelings and fears, and taking our safety seriously, developing physical strength is powerful.

Alarms   Cashing in on the market in women's fear, there are now a number of 'personal alarms' and other devices intended to scare off attackers available. Again, they have their limitations – if you have time to extract the device from your bag or pocket, you may be better off spending that time running. And there are cheaper alternatives – sports whistles to attract attention, and some women carry an aerosol or squeezy lemon to squirt in an attacker's eyes. These methods are intended to startle an attacker for just long enough for you to escape. It is illegal to carry anything that could be described as an 'offensive weapon'.

Group action   In a group of women you can do more to work against male violence. Whether you campaign for practical changes locally (better street-lighting, say) in the interests of safety, join or set up a rape crisis centre, protest about pornography or a judge's comments on a rape case, you will be bringing to public attention the real level of violence against women and the attitudes that allow and perpetuate it. Breaking the silence around the threat we live under as women is powerful – it is strengthening to all women and helps to place the responsibility where it belongs, with men.

The possibilities for group action are as endless as the problem. It is important however that any such action be undertaken within a supportive group of women who recognise the extent of male violence against women and the power structures that perpetuate that rather than as, say, an individual campaign against a particular man. Do not underestimate the resistance we meet when we decide to speak out and challenge the power of men to abuse us.

Local community groups   You may find tenants' groups, residents' associations, student unions etc. willing to take up issues around safety at night. If you have bad lighting in your street, block of flats, estate or college, harass landlords, council or college authorities until something is done about it.

You can also get together with other women in the area and either work as a group specifically around male violence (see WAVAW groups below) or as a general support group taking up issues as they arise. Particularly if there has been a series of rapes or attacks in your area, you should find plenty of women interested in action if you call a public meeting. Some ideas for discussion are:

(a) arranging a method of escorting or transporting women to their homes, or work if they work by nights;

(b) arranging an alarm system to alert the residents of a neighbourhood, e.g. whistles;

(c) getting to know immediate neighbours and working out an alarm system between yourselves;

(d) arranging a rota for picking up children from school or nursery;

(e) compiling details of attackers (e.g. car registration numbers of kerb crawlers, identities, if known, of attackers) and publishing it in a newsletter or local paper;

(f) making sure the local police are taking the problem seriously and are treating women who have been raped with respect;

(g) if a man has raped and not been arrested, and if the woman who has been attacked agrees, you could have posters with his photo and a description of the crime circulated;

(h) if judges have made contemptuous remarks or decisions, you could arrange a picket of their courts or home.

These suggestions mainly deal with the rapist who is a stranger. Many women and girls are, of course, raped by men known to them or closely related and often in the 'safety' of their own homes.

Women Against Violence Against Women (WAVAW) groups

There are many WAVAW groups, each independent, throughout the country. There is no central contact or list of groups – you can find out if there is one in your area from local women's centres or newsletters. If there is not you can advertise there for other women interested in setting one up.

Some of the action that WAVAW groups commonly take is set out below – you can, of course, organise such actions in any group of women – however, a national network of women working towards the same end under an easily identifiable name or banner has a more powerful effect in terms of public education. These are only some examples of ways women have used to fight back against male violence – there are many more and new ones are continually being evolved. All these methods need to be undertaken with care and as a group, preferably benefiting from the experiences of other groups as well.

Pickets of sex or porn shops and shows, sexually violent films, courts and trials where comments or assumptions offensive to women are being made. To organise an effective picket, you need placards stating clearly and simply the focus of the protest, leaflets to hand out to other women on the street and a press release explaining what you are doing and why. You may be moved on by the police but you do not have to give them your names.

Reclaim the night marches   Particularly useful in areas in which there have been attacks on women recently are all-women demonstrations, bringing women together in a large group to walk carrying placards and torches, and chanting together. You need to plan the route carefully, preferably with a hall or large open space to meet in at the beginning and end so that large crowds are not gathered in the street. You will also have to notify the police of your intention to march and they will doubtless accompany you in force.

Sit-ins   A group of women sits in at a sex shop, video shop selling sexually violent material, newspaper or other institution encouraging violence, to make a protest. If the police come and you move, they will not arrest you. If you refuse to move they will, which will get you more publicity and possibly a few days in gaol. Whichever way you choose, you need plenty of women.

Press releases and other media work   If you are organising any of the above it is worth writing a statement explaining what you are doing and why, and sending it to local and/or national papers and radio stations. Put the name of one member of your group and a contact phone number on it for further information and/or comment. This will get the group known and you may well be contacted by the press as issues arise, for your views. If you are prepared to give talks too, on radio or TV, or locally in schools, women's groups and so on, it is an excellent way of bringing to public attention the intolerable and generally accepted level of male violence against women.

Posters and stickers   Another way of drawing attention to 'normal' sexual violence is by placing stickers on offensive advertisements or cinema posters – for example, 'you call this art, we call it violence against women'. You can get your own printed. You can also protest officially about advertisements that use male violence against women by writing to the Advertising Standards Authority – it claims to take objections seriously but is a mostly male and fairly toothless body, which is likely to find justifiable or acceptable most of what we as women find objectionable.

Rape Crisis Centres

Each centre so far set up in the UK is run by an autonomous group. Although the priorities and politics vary to some extent, all the groups share a commitment to providing a service run by and for women. The idea emerged from women meeting and sharing their experiences, and rape crisis centres are firmly rooted in feminist analysis and practice. It is from this that the strength women gain from contacting an RCC derives – from the validation of their experiences by other women, from each woman's control over what contact she wishes to have, from access to information combined with a supportive, non-judgmental atmosphere in which to make decisions that are right for her.

If there is already a RCC in your area, they will probably run training courses for women wanting to join the group. If there is no centre locally and you have a group of women interested in starting one, below are a few notes based on the experience of the LRCC on how to go about it.

You need to decide what kind of service you can, and want to, provide – if there is as yet no help for women who have been raped in your area, anything you do will be a big step forward, even if you are not able to offer a 24-hour phone line to start with. You will have to tailor the service you can offer according to the time you have available and the other commitments you have. Decide on your priorities and attract other women to spread the workload.

The London Rape Crisis Centre – what we do

We started off over eight years ago as a small group of women who had full-time jobs and/or young children. Although we now have three full-time and two part-time paid workers and around 30 unpaid workers at the centre, during the planning stages we had to do everything in our spare time. It was only when we had managed to raise funds and find a house that the possibility of employing women became a reality. The paid workers take the phones between 10 am and 6 pm, Monday to Friday, and co-ordinate the work of the whole group, and unpaid workers take calls after 6 pm and at the weekends.

Most decisions on policy are made collectively at weekly meetings, and the whole group is closely involved with the running of the Centre. Roughly, the work we do at the Centre involves:

Counselling – by phone and face-to-face Some women call us immediately or soon after the rape – these calls may result in a whole morning's work if, say, VD and pregnancy referrals and legal information are needed, as well as someone to talk to. We also receive many calls from women who were raped months or years ago.

Offering a 24-hour counselling line means that whenever a woman makes the decision to contact us, there is always another woman for her to talk to. Her first contact with us is an important step in regaining the control over her life which the rape took from her, so we try to ensure that she has called because *she* wanted to, not because others have pressurised her into doing so. For this reason we do not take third party referrals – we will only make appointments for a woman, whether to see one of us or to attend clinics, and so on, if she herself asks us to do so. Although we offer support and information to friends and family who may be distressed themselves, we encourage them to give our number to the woman herself.

We receive many queries about legal and medical information from women. Others want to share thoughts and feelings about what has happened and how it has affected their lives. Most if not all of the conversations we have with women are a combination of both.

Women frequently begin calls with apologies. We do find it difficult to ask for our emotional needs to be met and we know that for the woman who phones, ringing us is a brave and positive step. A woman may think she should 'be over it by now' and be urged by family and friends to forget about the rape. We encourage women to share the feelings they actually have, rather than the feelings imposed on them by other people. It is important that we raise the possibility of pregnancy or venereal disease with a woman, generally on her first contact with us, and we offer to make medical referrals or appointments at clinics when necessary.

About half of our contacts with women are through a single confidential telephone call. Increasingly though, women are using the 24-hour telephone line on an ongoing basis and/or requesting face-to-face contact. With one-off telephone calls, a woman can hang up or end the call at any time. Ongoing work, however, is a commitment between two women, with the limits negotiated by each of them.

As well as acknowledging the power and truth of the experiences of individual women, it is important that we put those experiences into a political context. When counselling, we challenge the myths about rape which permeate our thinking and feelings to a frightening extent (see Chapter 1). All of us to some extent plan our lives around the threat of rape. By making connections between all of our experiences as women and girls and those of the women ringing us, we try to break down the isolation and silence that surrounds rape and sexual abuse. Talking about rape and sexual abuse is very upsetting and painful – we try to provide the necessary security and support to make it possible for the women who contact us. We do not want fear to be paralysing —it can be transformed to anger which is strengthening. Speaking out about rape and sexual abuse can give women and girls alike the courage and strength to carry on and to regain control over their lives.

Referrals and accompanying   We can arrange medical appointments or refer women to doctors or lawyers for appropriate advice. Housing problems may also arise and women can be referred to specialised agencies if necessary. We also go with women to police stations, court and clinics if they want us to.

Ongoing research   We continually collect information about services available locally for women who have been raped, and make contact with different organisations which might be useful.

Public education   We arrange for group members to talk to various organisations about our work, deal with requests from the media for information, comment and interviews, and respond to requests from the public and other organisations for published material and/or information about our work.

Research   We log all calls we receive and compile statistics monthly and annually of the women who contact us.

Fundraising, routine finance (accounts etc.) and general administrative work (typing, photocopying and so on).

How we began

We started off by meeting regularly to discuss rape in general terms, what rape involves, how it affected our lives, what it means to be a woman in this society, what we could do about rape etc. This was a fundamental and lengthy part of developing our aims, ways of working as a feminist collective and in particular what we meant by counselling.

Premises   We were fortunate to find a self-contained house with our own entrance. We have since discovered that many women who come to the centre need reassuring that they will not meet any men. We also learned that keeping the address confidential was essential, so our postal address is a P.O. box number. We receive many threats and take security very seriously.

Money   We applied for money from charitable trusts, government and local government bodies. First, we became a registered charity – many charitable trusts will not give money unless you are one. You need to work out a draft budget for your first year of operation before you start applying for funds. About three-quarters of the money we raise goes on salaries, the rest on running costs – rent, phones, heating, books, equipment, publicity, and so on.

Fund-raising is very difficult when you first start, but once you get someone to say they will fund you, it becomes easier to attract other funders. They always ask where else you are getting money from and seldom want sole responsibility.

Although we started off with two full-time workers who did every-thing, we soon found that fund-raising and finance was a full-time job in itself and as the workload increased we employed a third worker to undertake this.

Contacts   We met with and talked to lots of different groups and set up specific arrangements with some of them – for example, doctors, VD clinics, pregnancy and abortion agencies. Basically, we scoured London building up contacts for our resource file – law centres, housing agencies, hospitals, Samaritans, CABs, social workers, Women's Aid, women's centres, and local and national government councillors who would support funding applications.

We got local as well as national figures on rape so we could show the need in our area for a centre. We also had to show that what we were going to do would not duplicate any existing service, either statutory or voluntary. In making contacts with other agencies there-fore, we checked what they were doing, what their attitudes were, and their opening hours. This was useful information when we started, as well as to show funders the need for us.

Medical and legal information   As well as building up contacts we needed to have detailed information ourselves on medical and legal procedures. Many women who contact us may have VD, are pregnant, need an abortion, or have housing or legal problems arising from, or aggravated by, being raped. We are often asked specific questions and need to give clear answers and have local contacts to provide further information if necessary. We found out local facilities for VD testing, pregnancy testing, abortion, post-coital pregnancy prevention and learnt about procedures, side effects and contra-indications where appropriate. We gathered information on the legal process and made contact with sympathetic women solicitors and barristers whom we could get further information from when necessary. We found it very useful to attend at least one rape trial. As rape counsellors we often accompany women to court and found it important to know the procedure ourselves so that we can explain what is happening. We were quickly made aware of the lack of sympathy there is for women who have been raped.

The press and media   We have to be very careful about publicity; newspaper articles, TV and radio programmes easily distort things we say. We always get the name of the journalist, a phone number, whom they work for, and find out exactly what they want. We tell them we must discuss their proposition with the rest of the group and avoid getting trapped into off-the-cuff statements we may later regret. We ask to see articles or programmes before they go out and get an assurance that we can make changes if we disagree. We make sure we are paid – we need all the money we can get.

Emotional involvement and commitment   We came to realise that setting up a rape crisis centre involved a very high level of commitment. Each member of the group has a clear idea of what her personal commitment can reasonably be and the group works around each woman's availability. We became aware of the dangers of too much emotional involvement – working collectively, and with an emphasis on mutual support within the group, is helpful in sorting out problems.

Appendix 1: Research

Traditionally, academics have mystified the process of developing ideas and theories, separating it off into élite institutions, with special customs and language. Historically women have been the objects, not the instigators, of research.[1]

It is important to be clear about the way *we* use the term 'research', since in the past, 'academic research' has distorted and obscured facts and devalued our experience as women. We all live with the results of such research which deny our reality and define us as 'victims', 'seductresses' and 'liars'. Well-established academics have proclaimed themselves authorities on our feelings and experiences, and become 'established' off our backs. As individual women, our word has no credibility unless corroborated by (male) experts.

We see research as questioning established practice, as well as sharing and validating our experiences, naming them as real, and building them into our theory.

The tables on the following pages are a combination of the questions most often asked about rape and sexual assault, and a refutation of some of the more common myths.

Table 3: Type of attack

Sample: 495 women, 550 assaults (this discrepancy reflects the fact that some women suffer more than one kind of assault, e.g. abduction and rape)

	Number	Percentage
Rape	366	66.5
Indecent assault	46	8.4
Incest	15	2.8
Attempted rape	12	2.0
Buggery	11	2.0
Threatening behaviour	9	1.5
Child molestation	7	1.5
Assault	13	2.5
Abduction	3	0.5
Theft	3	0.5
Attempted murder	2	0.4
Indecent exposure	2	0.4
Obscene phone calls	2	0.4
Other	1	0.2
Unknown	58	10.5

For the purpose of these tables, the categories are based on the present legal definitions of sexual offences. The category 'other' includes crimes which at present have no legal definition – sexual harassment at work, obscene gestures, verbal harassment on the street, fears for women themselves, their friends or relatives.

Table 4: Multiple assailants

Sample: 51 (out of 550 attacks)

Number of assailants	Number of attacks
2	25
3	15
4	4
More than 4	7

Table 5: Relationship of assailant to woman

Sample: 281

Relationship	Number	Percentage
Stranger	128	46
Acquaintance	82	29
Position of trust	24	9
Known – friend	24	9
– lover/husband	13	4
– relative	10	3

Categories are defined as follows:

Stranger: assailant was completely unknown to the woman.

Acquaintance: some slight relationship had been established, whether over a short or long period of time.

Position of trust: assailant was social worker, milkman, electricity or gas man, doctor, therapist or other person with whom the woman had dealings in a formal or professional sense.

Friend: woman had known assailant for some time and felt she had a friendly relationship with him.

Lover/husband: consensual sexual relationship had preceded the assault.

Relative: assailant was related by blood or marriage to the woman. Over 50 percent of women knew their assailants to some degree, which refutes the widely held myth that rapists are strangers.

Table 6: Scene of assault

Sample: 221

Scene		Number	Percentage
Inside	– woman's home	69	31
	– assailant's home	39	18
	– other	24	11
Outside	– street	31	14
	– car/taxi	20	9
	– car park/garage	6	3
	– park/woods	17	8
	– other	15	7

This table explodes another myth: that all rapes happen in dark alleys. 60 percent of women were raped inside a building; 31 percent in their own homes. Official statistics would have us believe the myth, without considering that women may be less likely to report an assault that occurred in their own homes, especially by someone they knew.

Table 7: Age of women at time of assault

Sample: 195

Age	Percentage of total	Cumulative percentage
0 – 9	2	2
10 – 15	20	22
16 – 20	32	54
21 – 35	38	92
36 – 60	6	98
50+	2	100

It would be misleading to assume that these figures represent a definitive age distribution of women who are raped. They can, however, be taken as an indication of the age groups most likely to contact the London RCC, bearing in mind that slightly less than half the women who contact us do so within one week of the attack. 54 percent of the women who contact us are aged 20 or under.

Appendix 2:
Glossary of Legal Terms

Accomplice   A partner in crime.

Accused   The man who is being charged with the offence. He is known as 'the accused'.

Acquittal   Where the accused is found not guilty.

Bail   Release from prison or prison custody, pending trial; sometimes given on conditions. Failure to appear for trial is a criminal offence itself.

Barrister   The person who receives instructions from the solicitor and appears in court on behalf of the client to put the client's case.

Carnal knowledge   To have sexual intercourse with.

Civil law   Process by which grievances between individual private citizens are settled.

Complainant   The woman who reports a sexual assault to the police.

Conviction   Where the accused is found guilty by the jury, or pleads guilty.

Corroboration   Confirmation of a statement by evidence (known as corroborative evidence). Can be, for example, an eye-witness to a crime, or injuries to corroborate a charge of physical violence.

Counsel   Another name for barristers. Can be either 'prosecution counsel' or 'defence counsel' (see below).

Criminal law   Where the State disciplines the offender and therefore the Crown becomes the prosecutor (one party), and the offender is the other party. This applies to sexual offences, which is why the woman is only a witness and not one of the parties.

Cross-examination   The practice of questioning and cross-questioning by both sides of the court.

Defence   The 'side' belonging to the defendant, who must fight the charge(s) against him (by destroying the evidence that the prosecution produces).

Defendant   Same as the accused: the man who is defending himself against the charge.

Diet   English name for foreign parliamentary assemblies (Concise Oxford Dictionary); a hearing, in Scottish legal procedure.

Felony (archaic)   Crime considered especially grave, usually including violence.

Forensic   Used in a court of law (for example, forensic evidence).

Hearsay (evidence)   What is heard to have been said by another person, but is not known to be true.

In camera   In the judge's private chambers (at the back of the court) or not in open court.

Legal Aid   Government-funded, means-tested financial assistance to pay legal fees.

Misdemeanour (archaic)   Crime less serious than felony.

Plea   The defendant's answer to the charge(s) against him (he 'pleads guilty' or 'changes his plea').

Prosecution   The 'side' of a court case whose job it is to prove to the jury's satisfaction that the accused is guilty.

Sexual assault, sexual offence   Self-evident, though they have no strict legal meaning; the particular offence must be specified – rape, indecent assault, buggery, etc. – for it to appear as a charge.

Solicitor   The person who is legally qualified to advise clients and prepare cases for barristers. Also known as instructing solicitor.

Statutory   Actually written down in legislative form, as in an Act of Parliament (as opposed to *case* law, which is developed from individual court cases). Indecent assault has no statutory definition, but evolves from how different judges have chosen to define it in their own courts.

Unlawful sexual intercourse   Intercourse between people who are not married to each other; mainly used in law when the girl is under the age of consent.

Appendix 3: London Rape Crisis Centre Reading List

The London Rape Crisis Centre does not necessarily agree with the contents of articles and books on this list.

London RCC publications

First Report, 1977 RCRP, £1.00 plus p&p.
Second Report, 1978, RCRP, £1.00 plus p&p.
Third Report, 1982, RCRP, £1.00 plus p&p.
'Rape, Police & Forensic Practice', Oct 1978, RCRP, £1.00 plus p&p.
'RCRP submission to Criminal Law Revision Committee on Sexual Offences Law', Nov 1981, RCRP, £1.00 plus p&p.
Rape Crisis Centre Leaflet, RCRP, 4p per copy.
Rape & Fighting Back Leaflet, RCRP, 2½p per copy.

Books

Menachem Amir, *Patterns in Forcible Rape*, University of Chicago Press, Chicago, 1971.

Karen Adams & Jennifer Fay, *No More Secrets – Protecting your child from sexual assault*, Impact Publishers, California, 1981.

Maya Angelou, *I Know Why The Caged Bird Sings: a personal memoir*, Bantam Books, New York, 1969.

Kathleen Barry, *Female Sexual Slavery*, Prentice Hall Inc., New Jersey, 1979.

Susan Brownmiller, *Against Our Will – Men, Women & Rape*, Penguin, Harmondsworth, 1977.

Ann Burgess & Lynda Holstrom, *Rape: Victims of Crisis*, Robert J. Brady, Florida, 1977.

Ann Burgess *et al*, *Sexual Assault of Children and Adolescents*, Lexington, Massachusetts, 1978.

Lorene Clark & Debra Lewis, *Rape: The Price of Coercive Sexuality*, Toronto Women's Press, Toronto, 1977.

Andrea Dworkin, *Our Blood*, The Women's Press, London, 1981.

Andrea Dworkin, *Pornography: Men Possessing Women*, The Women's Press, London, 1981.

Susan Griffin, *Pornography & Silence*, The Women's Press, London, 1981.

Susan Griffin, *Rape: The Power of Consciousness*, Harper & Row, New York, 1978.

Judith Herman, *Father Daughter Incest*, Harvard University Press, Boston, 1981.

Elizabeth Hilberman, *The Rape Victim*, Basic Books Inc., New York, 1976.

HMSO, *Criminal Statistics for England & Wales*, out every August – statistics available on request from RCRP .

Laura Lederer (ed.), *Take Back the Night: Women on Pornography*, William Morrow & Co., New York, 1980.

Sarah Nelson, *Incest: Fact not Fiction*, Stramullion Press, Edinburgh, 1981.

Florence Rush, *The Best Kept Secret: Sexual Abuse of Children*, Prentice Hall Inc., New Jersey, 1980.

Diana Russell, *The Politics of Rape*, Stein & Day, New York, 1975.

Articles and Pamphlets

'Daddy Said Not To Tell: Dynamics of Child Sexual Assault', Radio interview with Barbara Meyers, reported in *Aegis Newsletter*, FAAR, Washington DC, Sept–Oct 1979.

Romi Bowen & Angela Hamblin, 'Sexual Abuse of Children', *Spare Rib*, no. 106, London, May 1981.

Helen Chetin, 'Francis Ann Speaks Out – My Father Raped Me', New Seed Press, California, 1977.

Susan Griffin, 'Rape: The all American Crime', *Ramparts*, vol. 10, no. 3, Know Inc, Pittsburgh, Ohio, Sept 1971.

Jenni Hall, 'Countering the Rape Myth', *Peace News*, Nottingham, June 1978.

Judith Herman & Lisa Hirschman, 'Father Daughter Incest: a Feminist Theoretical Perspective', *Signs*, Chicago, vol. 2, no. 4, Summer 1977.

HMSO, 'American Study of Female Sexuality' Report of the Advisory

Committee on the law on Rape (White Paper), Cmnd 3352, Dec 1975.

HMSO, *Sexual Offences Amendment Act 1976.*

Criminal Law Revision Committee, 'Working Paper on Sexual Offences Law', HMSO, Oct 1980.

Miriam Jackson, 'Incest: The Last Taboo', *Broadsheet*, Auckland, New Zealand, Nov 1979.

Charlotta Mitra, 'For She Has No Right or Power to Refuse Her Consent', *Criminal Law Review*, London, 30 Aug 1979.

Janice Reynolds, 'Rape as Social Control', *Telos*, Department of Sociology, Washington University, St Louis, Missouri.

Florence Rush, 'The Sexual Abuse of Children', Vol 18, *Journal of Child Psychology & Psychiatry*, U.S., vol. 21, 1980.

To obtain London Rape Crisis Centre publications and for information on obtaining pamphlets, please write to: London Rape Crisis Centre, P.O. Box 69, London WC1X 9NJ.

Books are available by mail order from: Compendium, 234 Camden High Street, London NW1; Sisterwrite, Upper Street, London N1. The latter produce a catalogue of available titles.

Appendix 4: List of Rape Crisis Centres, May 1983

London, open 24 hrs. Tel: 01-837 1600; P.O. Box 69, London WC1X 9NJ.

Aberdeen, Mon 6–8 pm, Thurs 7–9 pm. Tel: 0224–575560, 24 hr answering; P.O. Box 123, Aberdeen.

Belfast, Tues & Fri 7 pm–10 pm. Tel: 0232–249696; P.O. Box 46, Belfast BT2 7AR.

Birmingham, open 24 hrs. Tel: 021–233 2122; P.O. Box 558, Birmingham B3 2HI.

Bradford, Mon 1–5 pm, Thurs 6–10 pm. Tel: 0274–308270, 24 hr answering; P.O. Box 155, Bradford BD5 7PW.

Brighton, Tues 6–9 pm, Fri 3–9 pm, Sat 10–1 pm. Tel: 0273–699756, P.O. Box 332, Hove, East Sussex BN3 BX3.

Cambridge, Wed 6–12 pm, Sat 11 am–5 pm. Tel: 0223–358314, 24 hr answering.

Cleveland, Thurs 7–10 pm. Tel: 0642–813397, 24 hr answering; P.O. Box 31, Middlesborough, Cleveland.

Cork, Mon 7.30–10 pm, Wed 2–5 pm, Fri 10 am–1 pm, Sat 10 am–4 pm. Tel: 968086; P.O. Box 42, Brian Borr Street, Cork.

Coventry, Mon 11 am–3 pm, 7 pm–10 pm, Tues–Fri 11–3 pm. Tel: 0203–77229; P.O. Box 76, Coventry CV1 2QS.

Dublin, Mon–Fri 8 pm–8 am, Sat & Sun 24 hrs. Tel: 0001–601470; P.O. Box 1027, Dublin 6.

Edinburgh, Mon & Wed 1–2, 6–8 pm, Thurs 7–10 pm, Fri 6–8 pm. Tel: 031–556 9437; P.O. Box 120 Head P.O., Edinburgh, EH1 3ND.

Highlands (*Inverness*), Mon 6–8 pm, Thurs 7–9 pm. Tel: 0463–220719; c/o The Women's Group, IVOG Ardconnell St., Inverness.

Leeds, 10 am–12 pm 7 days a week. Tel: 0532–440058, 0532–441323 office. P.O. Box 27, Leeds LS2 7EG.

Leicester, Tues 7–10 pm, Sat 2–5 pm. Tel: 0533–666 666.

Liverpool, Mon 7–9 pm, Thurs & Sat 2–5 pm. Tel: 051–734 4369, 24 hr answering.

Manchester, Tues 2–5 pm, Thurs 7–9 pm, Fri 2–5 pm, Sun 6–8 pm. Tel: 061–228 3602, 061–228 0619 office, 24 hr answering; P.O. Box 336, Manchester M60 2B5.

Norwich, Mon & Thurs 7–10 pm, Fri 11 am–2 pm. Tel: 0603–667687, 24 hr answering; c/o Resource Centre, P.O. Box 47, Norwich, NR1 2BU.

Nottingham, Mon–Fri 11–5 pm. Tel: 0602–410440 (separate line at women's centre); P.O. Box 37a, Mansfield Road, Nottingham.

Oxford women's line, Wed 2–10 pm. Tel: 0865–726295, 24 hr answering; P.O. Box 73, Oxford OX3 6E2.

Portsmouth, Wed & Sat 7–10 pm, Fri 7 pm–7 am, Sun 3 pm–6 pm. Tel: 0705–669511, 24 hr answering.

Reading, Sun 7.30–10.30 pm. Tel: 0734–55577, 24 hr answering; P.O. Box 9, 17 Chatham Street, Reading.

Sheffield, Mon & Fri 10 am–1 pm, Thurs 8–10 pm, Sat 12–3 pm. Tel: 0742–755 255, 24 hr answering; P.O. Box 34, Sheffield 1.

South Wales, Mon & Thurs 7–10 pm, Wed 11 am–2 pm. Tel: 0222–373181, 24 hr answering.

Strathclyde, Mon, Wed & Fri 7–10 pm. Tel: 041–221 8448, 24 hr answering; P.O. Box 53, Glasgow 2.

Tyneside, Weekdays 10–10 pm, Sat & Sun 6.30–10 pm. Tel: 0632–329858, 24 hr answering; P.O. Box 13, Gosforth, Newcastle upon Tyne.

Appendix 5: Pregnancy and Abortion – Useful Agencies

1. Brook Advisory Centres

These are charities set up in 1963 to help young people. They now offer a free service to under-25-year-olds for contraception but see women of any age for pregnancy advice and post-coital contraception. Where abortion is indicated, referral is usually made to National Health Service hospitals.

There are Brook Advisory Centres all over the country. To find out where your nearest one is, you can telephone or write to their head office at 153a East Street, London SE17 2SD. Tel: 01–708 1234.

2. Abortion charities

These are charities which offer pregnancy advice and post-coital contraception. They will refer women who want abortions to private clinics which specialise in this area. They normally charge fees.

Pregnancy Advisory Service 11–13 Charlotte Street, London W1P 1HD. Tel: 01–637 8962.
Open: Mon–Thurs 9.30 am–5.30 pm; Saturday (pregnancy testing only) 10 am–12 am; Thursday (late pregnancy testing only) 5.30 pm–7.30 pm.
Fees (should be checked as they change regularly):
    Early pregnancy test (14 days after suspected conception) £5
    Urine pregnancy test (2 weeks after missed period) £2
    Post-coital contraception (Morning after pill – taken up to 72 hours after unprotected intercourse) £15

Abortions: consultation £20
up to 12 weeks £95
12 to 18½ weeks £120
They will refer women to other agencies for later abortions.

British Pregnancy Advisory Service[BPAS] This organisation has branches all over the country and is the oldest charity in the country dealing with problems of fertility and infertility. To find your local branch, either write to or ring their head office at Austy Manor, Wootton Wawen, Solihull, West Midlands B95 6BX. Tel: Henley in Arden 3225.

Fees (should be checked as they change regularly):
Pregnancy test (9 days after missed period) £3
Morning after pill (up to 72 hours after intercourse) £21
Abortion: up to 14 weeks £100 + consultation fee £21
14 to 19 weeks £200 + consultation fee £21
19 to 22 weeks £252 + consultation fee £21

Pregnancy and Gynaecological Advisory Service This agency is a private business and is not a charity. However their fees are similar to those charged by the charities and they are the only ones who do abortions after 22 weeks. They do not charge a consultation fee which means that if you are not pregnant, or if you decide not to have an abortion you will not have to pay. They also have a loan scheme whereby they can lend money to women who need abortions and who have none. The loan scheme is backed by a charitable fund to which they have access.

Pregnancy and Gynaecological Advice Service[P&GAS] 26 Fauberts Place, London W1. Tel: 01-437 7125.
Open: Mon–Fri 9 am–5.30 pm; Sat 9 am–1 pm; telephone answering service Mon–Fri until 7.30 pm.
Fees (should be checked as they change regularly):
Pregnancy test (2 weeks after missed period) £3
Abortions: up to and including 14 weeks £125
15–19 weeks £155
19–20 weeks £220
20–24 weeks (1 stage) £220
(2 stage) £300
After 16 weeks you may need a scan which can cost £25.

P&GAS do not do prostaglandin induction (see Chapter 6, Abortion Methods). After 19 weeks they do a D & C type operation which may involve one general anaesthetic or two depending on how big the foetus is. This is much less upsetting than prostaglandin induction which is the method used by all other agencies (including NHS) for abortions over 16 weeks.

3. Adoption and fostering

British Adoption and Fostering Service (BAAF is an umbrella organ-isation which co-ordinates the work of all fostering and adoption agencies (both statutory and voluntary) in Great Britain. They can provide you with a list of adoption and fostering agencies free of charge. There are many such agencies in Great Britain. Some offer accommodation to women who are pregnant during the period of confinement (six weeks before and six weeks after the birth). Some offer support to women who choose to keep their babies – some do not. It is worth checking in advance exactly what they offer.
BAAF, 11 Southwark Street, London SE1. Tel: 01-407 8800.

4. Single parents

National Council of One Parent Families, 255 Kentish Town Road, London NW5 2LX. Tel: 01–267 1361. Open: Mon–Fri 9.15 am–5.15 pm.
Offers free advice and information to all lone parents and is also a campaigning group.

Notes

Chapter 1: pages 1–7

1. London Rape Crisis Centre, *Third Report*, 1982.
2. Reprinted from *War on Rape*, War on Rape Collective, Melbourne, Australia, 1977.
3. *Home Office Criminal Statistics for England and Wales*, HMSO, 1980.
4. Vincent de Francis (ed.), *Sexual Abuse of Children*, Children's Division of the American Humane Association, Denver, 1967.
5. Menachim Amir, *Patterns in Forcible Rape*, University of Chicago Press, 1971; London Rape Crisis Centre, *First Report*, 1977.
6. London Rape Crisis Centre, 'Rape, Police and Forensic Practice', 1979.
7. 'If a woman walks into a police station and complains of rape with no signs of violence she must be closely interrogated. Allow her to make her statement to a policewoman, and then drive a horse and cart through it. It is always advisable if there is any doubt of the truthfulness of her allegations to call her an outright liar. It is very difficult for a person to put on genuine indignation who has been called a liar to her face. . . Watch out for the girl who is pregnant or late getting home at night, such persons are notorious for alleging rape or indecent assault. Do not give her sympathy. If she is not lying, after the interrogator has upset her by accusing her of it, then at least the truth is verified and the genuine complaint made by her can be properly investigated.' *Police Review*, 28 Nov 1975.
8. *Outwrite* (issue 7, Oct 1982) reported a case in the USA recently where the parents of a lesbian arranged for her to be systematically raped to 'de-programme' her.

Chapter 3: pages 24–37

1. Charlotta Mitra, 'For She has no Right or Power to Refuse her Consent', *Criminal Law Review*, 30 Aug 1979.
2. *Working Paper on Sexual Offences*, HMSO, 1980.

3. Severely subnormal, as defined in the Mental Health Act 1959.

4. *Home Office Criminal Statistics for England and Wales*, HMSO, 1980.

5. *Ibid.*

6. *Ibid.*

7. *Ibid.*

8. *Ibid.*

9. *Ibid.*

10. This involved the defendant Morgan, who, while drinking with three male acquaintances, invited them back to his house for sex with his wife. She might, he said, scream, shout and protest, but they should take no notice since this was her way of getting aroused; she would really be enjoying it. All four then went to Morgan's home where, under much obvious protest, the three acquaintances proceeded to rape Mrs Morgan. All three were found guilty of rape and sentenced to four years each. Morgan got seven years as an accomplice. On appeal the convictions and sentences were upheld, but the three acquaintances were given leave to appeal to the House of Lords on a point of law, that since they *honestly believed* Mrs Morgan was consenting, they were not guilty of rape.

Although the Law Lords upheld the convictions, they reduced the sentences by one year, and made the *Morgan* ruling.

11. The only sexual offence by law requiring corroboration is procuration, a charge rarely brought. The Home Office states that '. . . "procuration", "abduction", "bigamy", and "gross indecency with a child" (together) . . . account for only 3–4 percent of convictions recorded. . .' (*Sexual Offences, Consent and Sentencing*, HMSO, 1979). They are considered to be 'less serious offences'.

12. Archbold, *Criminal Pleading Evidence and Practice*, 40th ed., p. 1415. (Archbold is one of the bibles of the legal profession.)

13. Judge Rigg, Central Criminal Court, Old Bailey, London, 1975.

14. Section 4, Sexual Offences Amendment Act 1976. The judge may allow such information to be admitted if he thinks that the accused's situation is likely to be prejudiced by excluding it, or that revealing it will induce likely *defence* witnesses to come forward (defence witnesses being, of course, for the man, and against the woman).

15. And other crimes defined as rape offences, but not any other sexual offences.

16. Section 4, Sexual Offences Amendment Act 1976.

17. See Zsuzsanna Adler, 'The Reality of Rape Trials', *New Society*, 4 Feb 1982.

Chapter 4: pages 38–53

1. Reprinted from *American Bar Association Journal*, vol. 61, Apr 1975.

2. London Rape Crisis Centre, *Third Report*, 1982.

3. 'Statements from females re sexual or indecency offences should if possible be taken by a female officer – otherwise have another constable present.' (Baker & Wilkie's Police Promotion Handbook No. 2, *Criminal Evidence and Procedure*, 6th ed., 1979, p. 121.)

4. See 'Rape, Police and Forensic Practice', London Rape Crisis Centre, 1978.

5. Baker & Wilkie's Police Promotion Handbook, p. 122.

6. *Ibid.*, p. 160.

7. 'Rape, Police and Forensic Practice', London Rape Crisis Centre.

Chapter 5: pages 54–66

1. Magistrates' Courts Act 1980.

2. *Ibid.*

3. *Ibid.*

4. 15 in Scotland.

5. If you do, the statement can be made a defence exhibit and shown to the jury. Your evidence may also be seen as less valid, the assumption being that if it is all true, you will remember everything properly.

6. All figures from *Home Office Criminal Statistics for England and Wales*, HMSO, 1980.

7. Criminal Injuries Compensation Scheme, 1979, Scheme B, para. 6.

8. Unless the Board have acted beyond their powers or have misinterpreted the scheme. If so, you have to apply to the Divisional Court (High Court) to review the Board's decision.

9. Criminal Injuries Compensation Scheme, 1979, Scheme B, paras. 6 and 7.

10. *Bulletin of Northern Ireland Law,* no. 6, 1981.

Chapter 6: pages 67–86

1. These figures were obtained by the Brook Advisory Centre in London from a study of 700 women. For more information on the 'morning after' pill, see *Women and the Crisis in Sex Hormones*, B. Seaman & G. Seaman, Harvester Press, Brighton, 1978.

2. G.M.C. Ethical Committee: Professional Conduct and Discipline: Fitness to Practice: August 1983.

Chapter 7: pages 87–108

1. Vincent de Francis (ed.), *Sexual Abuse of Children*, Children's Division of the American Humane Association, Denver, 1967.

Chapter 8: pages 109–114

1. *Sexual Harassment at Work*, Ann Sedley & Melissa Benn, NCCL Rights for Women Unit, 1982.

Appendix 1: page 127

1. For further discussion, see M. Daly, *Gyn/Ecology*, The Women's Press, London, 1979; A. Rich, *On Lies, Secrets and Silence*, Virago, London, 1980.

The Women's Press is a feminist publishing house. We aim to publish a wide range of lively, provocative books by women, chiefly in the areas of fiction, literary history, art history, physical and mental health and politics.

We can supply books direct (please add 35 pence for postage and packing) but please support our efforts to have our books available in all bookshops, libraries and educational institutes. To receive our complete list of titles please send a large stamped addressed envelope. We welcome suggestions and comments.

2'